(I most likely wouldn't have survived Guatemala without Barbara!

Margarita
A Guatemalan Peace Corps Experience

*"Use what talents you have;
if only the birds that sang sweetly
lifted their voices,
the woods would be silent."*
—AUTHOR UNKNOWN

Marjorie DeMoss Casebolt

RED APPLE PUBLISHING • GIG HARBOR, WASHINGTON

FIRST EDITION

 RED APPLE
PUBLISHING
15010 113th St. KPN
Gig Harbor, WA 98329-5014
(253) 884-1450

Printed by Gorham Printing
Rochester, WA 98579

ISBN 1-880222-38-8

Library of Congress Control Number 00-131293

Cover design by Kathy Campbell

Back cover photo by Marjorie DeMoss Casebolt

To My Father

Guatemala

YUCATÁN PENINSULA (MEXICO)

Petén

MEXICO

BELIZE

Atlantic Ocean

Puerto Barrios

Lake Izabal

Cobán

• Huehuetenanago

•Copán

HONDURAS

• Chichicastenango

Sololá
Lake
Atitlán
•Panajachel   • San Juan Sacatepéquez
                   Antigua   Guatemala City
San   • Matequescuintla •Jalapa
Antonio   Monjas
Palopó   Santa Lucia   Llano
                 Milpas Altas   Grande
Ciudad Vieja

        Escuintla
                              Zapatitlán

                   •Taxisco

        Monterrico

        EL SALVADOR

Pacific Ocean

◄GUATEMALA CITY   ▲
                   JALAPA

Carmen• Monjas•
Llano Grande •Terrones
River
•Piedra
del   River   Rinconada
Fuego

Preface

In the 1960s, after reading in the *National Geographic* about the work of a Peace Corps couple in South America, I knew that was something I wanted to do. Nearly thirty years later, after my four sons had finished college and were on their own, I applied and was accepted as a volunteer. Hoping to be sent to Africa, I envisioned myself living at a girls' school where I would teach home economics.

In 1988, I was assigned to serve in Guatemala as a nutritionist. I had visited there twice before, once taking a two-week Spanish class. Because neither my name, Marjorie, nor Marge, as I'm generally called, translate into Spanish, I became *Margarita*, which was what everyone called me.

Some of my friends have informed me I talk too much about food. However, as a teacher, I found food demonstrations a good way to teach nutrition. Besides, I love to cook, and my students enjoy sampling!

In my two years of living and working in a small village on the eastern border of Guatemala, I felt totally accepted, appreciated, and wanted. I look back on that time as one of the best in my life. A friend asked me why, and I responded, "It was because of the wonderful people."

—MDC

Foreword

In the late 1980s, when my husband, Barry, and I jumped off of our career ladders to join the Peace Corps, we imagined we'd be among the oldest volunteers, having obtained master's degrees and worked for several years first. We were pleasantly surprised, however, to find a collection of able-bodied and spirited seniors in our training group and the training groups that would follow our arrival in Guatemala.

Among the most inspirational was Marge Casebolt. She arrived a few months after we set up housekeeping in the city of Jalapa. We and the other volunteers enjoyed most creature comforts—indoor plumbing, electricity, and regular *chicken buses* to the capital, Guatemala City. Marge was stationed perhaps an hour south of Jalapa in the small, impoverished village of Llano Grande. Depending on the season, Marge's rural environs were either a dust bowl or a muddy pig wallow. When her local *chicken bus* wasn't running, this seasoned world traveler and mother of four outdoor-adventurer sons would hike the several miles to the main road in her Birkenstocks, often in the dark of early day. It wasn't difficult for Marge to hasten herself out of her flea-ridden bed because starting at 4:00 A.M. most mornings the church would blast evangelical music over a loudspeaker.

We all suffered from one parasite or another, but Marge was always matter-of-fact about hers, and she maintained the perspective all volunteers should have: "What have I to complain about. Peace Corps will tell me which drugs to use, and I'll be well in a couple of days. I am not a mother watching child after child die of malnutrition or dysentery."

Marge hiked into the isolated mountain villages to give *charlas* (talks) about nutrition and general health promotion, no mean feat for someone

7

just starting to learn Spanish. She effectively used her background as a home economist to give cooking and craft demonstrations and to promote breast feeding as a healthy and safe alternative to mixing formula with water absolutely alive with dangerous microorganisms.

I built an oven for one of Marge's women's groups so that she could teach bread-baking and possibly help them establish a small business making fresh loaves instead of buying stale bread brought to them from the city. Marge and I both fear that that oven now serves as a chicken coop.

My husband and I came to know Marge over the year and a half that our duties overlapped. She was a frequent houseguest, whose visits (and cooking) we enjoyed immensely. I am delighted beyond words that our dear friend has published *Margarita*, the fascinating account of her time in Guatemala.

—June Wiaz, Tallahassee, Florida

Who's Who

PEACE CORPS VOLUNTEERS:
Liesl (*nutritionist*), *assigned to
    Matequescuintla*
Liz, *agriculture volunteer at
    Matequescuintla site*
June and Barry (*appropriate
    technology*), *lived Jalapa*
Trina (*nurse*) and Gary (*agriculture*),
    *lived and worked in the mountains
    between Jalapa and Llano Grande*
Buck (*nutrition*)

STAFF:
Mario, *health and nutrition*
Sergio, *supervisor for health and nutrition*
Todd, *on training staff*

MY HOUSEHOLD:
(WHILE AT THE TRAINING CENTER)
Estella, *landlady*
Manuel Sr., *husband*
Five children

4-H:
Barbara
Marion
Kelly

MY HOUSEHOLD:
(IN LLANO GRANDE)
Chusita, *landlady*
Moses, *husband*
Cristobal, *brother*
Arnoldo, *nephew*
Grandma, *mother-in-law*
Eight children
Alicia, *helper and religious education
    director at church*
Goody-Two-Shoes, *helper*

HEALTH CENTER:
Linda, *nurse, married to Alfonso, uncle of
    Carlito*
Doctors: Sarita, Cézar, Servet, Roxane

TOWNSPEOPLE:
Maria, *4-H leader*
Leaders of women's groups:
    Olillia, Petronia, Elenora,
    Incarnation, Conception, Macaria
Nixon, *a two-year-old child*
Rosa, *Nixon's mother*
Paulina, *mother of eight
    malnourished children*
Pablo, *minister*
Eloisa, *his wife*

9

October 1988

On schedule, the Boeing jet left the Seattle-Tacoma airport, where I said good-bye to two of my four grown sons and three close family friends. I was sixty-two, newly divorced after forty years of marriage, and committed to serving for two years as a nutritionist with the Peace Corps in Guatemala.

After an interview with the Peace Corps office in Seattle the previous February, filling out pages of questions, sending in names of eight people for references, extensive physical and dental checks, and numerous telephone conversations to the office in Washington, D.C., in July, I learned I had been selected. In mid-September, I received a letter telling me I would be serving in Guatemala and to report to Miami on October 28.

Friends and family helped me close my waterfront home in Gig Harbor, Washington, [to be rented out], and we packed all my belongings in the downstairs den. My best friend had offered to handle mail, bills, investments, taxes and anything else needing attention.

On paper my qualifications looked good. Because my degree is in home economics, I had taught consumer education through a vocational school to low-income adults, had taught special education on a junior high level, and had acquired some skills in gardening. I knew a little Spanish, but my biggest uncertainty was whether or not I could communicate in Spanish and if I could live by myself in another country. I had traveled to a number of Third World countries and knew a little of what to expect, but a big doubt remained, along with a lump in my stomach. The government was about to spend a considerable sum of money on my training, and I planned to succeed. (Although it depends on the country, it costs around $15,000

11

to train a volunteer.)

I visited Peace Corps friends in Denver, who had recently served in Zaire, and spent the rest of the week in Connecticut with my oldest son and his family before flying to Iowa City where I had been awarded a scholarship for a week of Maternal and Child Nutrition update at the university.

My last stop was in West Palm Beach, Florida, to stay with a cousin who then drove me to Miami for "staging," the final step in the Peace Corps before leaving the country.

As I checked in at the Miami Hilton, I met a young woman with a Southern accent who introduced herself as "Joan" and suggested we have lunch together. Somehow I managed to get six pieces of luggage to my room. I seemed to be the only person bringing a portable typewriter in addition to two suitcases, a frame backpack and a day pack containing a camera, lenses, shortwave radio and tape deck, plus a purse.

After lunch with Joan and a young man from Georgia, my roommate arrived. Connie had been reared on an Ohio farm. She informed me she would be working in vegetable production and had majored in Spanish in college, adding that anyone who wasn't fluent would have a very difficult time.

That afternoon our training group gathered to introduce ourselves. We numbered fifty-seven and ranged in age from twenty-one to seventy. Nine of us were over fifty. I was given a color-coded tag that said "Nutrition." Other tags said Bee Keeping, Vegetable Production, Grain Storage, Crop Diversification, 4-H, and Youth Development.

During the three days in Miami we had talks from Peace Corps, Washington; lectures on safety and health; and took part in skits—such as boarding and riding a Guatemalan bus, to impress upon us how crowded we would find public transportation.

A delightful young African-American woman serving in the nutrition program shared her experiences. As a group we visited the Dade County Health Department for inoculations against measles, mumps, cholera, tetanus, polio and diphtheria.

Two nights before we were to leave was Halloween, and the streets were full of young people in costumes. It seemed strange, for we were all so focused on our unusual undertaking that none of us had given Halloween a thought.

November 1988

$\mathcal{T}$he group boarded a Pan Am plane for Guatemala City. On our arrival we were greeted by whoops and cheers from a number of volunteers who had come to the capital to welcome us and undoubtedly look over the field for the dating game. Strong arms relieved me of my luggage, and we were taken to a modest downtown hotel for the night. I shared a room with two young women—Cindy from North Carolina, whose accent was difficult for me to understand, and Sara from Vermont. Cindy was a nurse and in my program and Sara would work in 4-H.

At the hotel were the last hot showers and toilet seats we would see for a long time.

IT TOOK A LITTLE OVER AN HOUR by bus to get from Guatemala City to the training center in the mountains, about ten kilometers from Antigua, Guatemala's old capital. We drove on a modern highway past old towns, coffee farms called *fincas* and woodlands.

Our destination was Santa Lucia Milpas Altas, "the high cornfields at Saint Lucy," which nestled in a rich valley surrounded by hills, some forested and some cultivated. Vegetables such as snow peas, carrots and cabbages grow lushly on the slopes in the fertile volcanic soil. To the south and west are three volcanoes—Agua and Fuego, twelve thousand feet, and Acatenango, a thousand feet higher. There was enough rain that vegetation stayed green and crops were harvested year round.

The training center consisted of two long cement-block buildings facing each other across a green lawn. The wide, covered porches were hung

Barbara, Margarita and other volunteers

with fuchsia baskets. One side held offices and the other a cafeteria and meeting rooms. There were two bathrooms with flush toilets and warnings in both Spanish and English posted over the sinks that said, "Do not drink this water." Behind the buildings were solar showers, garden plots, animal pens, and small cabins for Spanish classes. Large glass containers on the porches held bottled water that was safe to drink.

Because our group was so large, we were divided for living quarters in three communities. Most of the older trainees stayed in town, and the younger ones stayed forty-five minutes to an hour or more across the highway and up a mountain on foot.

I was taken to my new home about four blocks away and introduced to my family. Estella, the mother, was a thin, young woman in her early thirties with the classic features of the Mayan Indians: high cheekbones, dark eyes and hair, and light coffee-colored skin. The five black-eyed children eyed me shyly. They all appeared small for their ages—Manuel, named for his father, was ten; Alex, nearly eight, the same age as my grandson; Rodolfo, five; impish Irving, three; and Ingred, not quite two.

This was the poorest house I had ever been in. Located on the corner of unpaved, dusty streets, the outside was a dirty yellow stucco with a yard enclosed with barbed wire. Owners of neighboring houses had made an

14

attempt to plant flowers, shrubs or vegetables. Aside from a pot of red geraniums, there were only a few avocado and coffee trees and a nespiro, which I learned was a type of small tropical plum.

I entered the dining room which contained a table, wooden chairs, and a large chest that seemed to hold most of their belongings. Beyond was a small bedroom with a three-quarter bed for Estella and her husband and Ingred and Irving's metal crib. Next was a tiny kitchen containing an apartment-size gas propane stove and a few shelves for dishes and food. Everything was stained, dusty, and dirty. The ceilings were beaver board and plastic tarp secured with rope.

The family had reserved a room for me next to the older boys', which was divided by a gunnysack curtain. It was furnished with a single bed, a dresser, and a table and chair. The floor was tile. The children watched as I spread my inflatable air mattress over the cornhusk pad, fitted clean sheets, used a down sleeping bag for my blanket, and a pillow from home. Estella provided a red chenille bedspread.

Lunch consisted of nearly unchewable fried beef, boiled macaroni, radishes and tortillas. Flies were everywhere; the only time I had seen more was when I was in Africa visiting a pitiful Maasi village in Tanzania. Later, it occurred to me that nearly all beef there is extremely tough and that the meal was a real splurge for this poor family.

In the backyard was a latrine constructed of concrete blocks surrounding a seatless toilet flushed by pouring water from a bucket. My hostess handed me a piece of newspaper, for which I thanked her, but showed her I carried Kleenex in my pocket. I had done enough traveling to know toilet paper in the Third World is non-existent.

Returning to the training center, I was joined by two other women. Barbara Hansen, four years older than I, was a Scandinavian originally from Minnesota now living in Lafayette, Louisiana. Barbara was easy-going and pleasant. Marion, our oldest trainee, was seventy years old, a small neat woman also from Minnesota, whose expertise had been teaching art in special education. Both women were working in the 4-H program with girls. We decided to meet after class to compare living quarters.

Back at the center I was gratified to have received some mail, including my absentee ballot for the Bush/Dukakis presidential election in which pro-choice had been made a political issue. I had until Monday to decide whether or not I could support the Republicans.

Our training, we were told, would cover three areas: Spanish, our work-related group, and "core," which included an understanding of the culture, safety, and health instruction. The woman in charge of the Spanish Department quizzed each of us to determine our fluency or lack of it.

The three of us visited Barbara's house located a block and a half from mine. She had a nice family of three teenage girls, a boy who attended high school in Antigua, and a very sick looking two-year-old. The place was considerably cleaner than mine and appeared better organized.

Marion lived farther down the street in a little house set back among trees and flowers. Her hosts were a young indigenous couple with children aged six months to five years. The husband worked as an agricultural representative for the government and proudly presented to us one of his programs on soil erosion.

THE FIRST MORNING IN MY NEW HOME I was issued a wake-up call at 3:30 A.M. by the family rooster. By 5:30, I was wide awake and pleased to have had Estella heat water for me for a bath. Behind the kitchen was a dirty storeroom piled high with junk. There were boxes where chickens roosted, several machetes, and bags of corn. A shower

A pila, *a three-sectioned tub used for almost everything*

16

consisted of pouring water over myself, and the floor was so filthy I made a mental note to purchase some thongs. Breakfast consisted of sweetened water for instant coffee, a thin watery oatmeal called *atol*, also sweetened, and a banana.

We had been warned never to drink untreated water in Guatemala, and I brushed my teeth with water from a plastic bottle in which I had dropped an iodine tablet. In the house there was no running water, but outside was a *pila* resembling a three-sectioned laundry tub. The middle was filled with clean but not potable water from a faucet or, when city water was shut off, carried in buckets. The other tubs were shallow with drains and used for tooth brushing as well as the washing of hands, clothes, small children, dishes, food and hair.

At SCHOOL OUR NUTRITION GROUP met our trainer, Mario, a young Guatemalan doctor who had done graduate work in Texas. Our class consisted of Andrew, a New Yorker, about forty with a master's degree in public health; Stephanie, twenty-nine, a registered dietitian from Michigan; Nori, the same age, also a dietitian from California; and Christine, a health teacher from Florida. The two young women were Cindy, the nurse I had roomed with who was from North Carolina, and Ellen, a strawberry blond who explained she had grown up in an orphanage in Indiana and then received a scholarship to a private Oregon college where she had majored in women's studies. There were two native Spanish speakers: Ana, a Cuban woman about thirty, with a degree in nutrition from Texas, and Maria, a stunning Mexican beauty, who held U.S. citizenship and had worked in food services in the Southwest.

Mario explained in good, but accented, English what we would be doing. We would weigh and measure children to assess their growth and learn to recognize severe malnutrition in order to get the child to the proper health facility. "Eighty percent of the children here are malnourished," he said, "but much of it can be prevented with proper diet and good prenatal care." In addition, we would learn how to grow vegetables in order to encourage people to establish their own gardens, as well as to improve their diets.

These were the things I had hoped we would do. Armed with a vocabulary list of Spanish phrases to study over the weekend, including the

17

names of twenty tools useful for vegetable production, I collected Marion and Barbara and we took the bus to Antigua, thirty minutes away.

We ate lunch at a lovely restaurant with an open patio that had been a magnificent home when Antigua was the capital of Guatemala and second in size to Mexico City. A series of devastating earthquakes had destroyed convents, old churches and a university. With its cobblestone streets, a beautiful park, trees and gardens, and good restaurants, it is like no other place in the country.

I bought a children's book in Spanish to read to my new family, a cantaloupe (melón in Spanish) to share, and a supply of toilet paper.

Back in Santa Lucia the family duck waddled into my room while I memorized the words in Spanish for rake, hoe, and pick ax. Dinner was a tamal and black beans. The tamal Estella had bought and consisted of a lump of unidentifiable meat or gristle (pork, chicken or turkey) covered with hot sauce, enclosed in tortilla dough, wrapped in banana or canna lily leaves, and steamed for several hours. After dinner I was shown pictures of the children when they were small, and in my poor Spanish I told them about my four sons and two grandchildren.

Estella told me about the Peace Corps volunteer who had left the month before. David (pronounced Dave-éd, with a long e) was young, from Oregon and had been an ideal guest. All of us, including the baby Ingred, drank sweet black coffee with our dinner, but I noticed she liked to nurse before she left the table.

Sunday morning I was again awakened by the rooster at 3:30. After breakfast, Barbara and Marion and I headed for the Antigua hotel where for $7.50 we could have a buffet dinner, swim, sun ourselves by a lovely pool, and study vocabulary. In contrast to our own living conditions, we had access to a hot shower where we were able to wash our hair.

That evening all five children watched as I typed a letter. Their mother had taught them to say, "*Con permiso*" (with permission), before they entered my room. Later, I could hear them playing typing as they sang, "ta ta ta ta ding!"

On MONDAY, TRAINING BEGAN in earnest and I awoke with a rotten cold. The group had the first of two rabies shots which Kathy, the head nurse, informed us cost the government $72.00 apiece.

18

Spanish classes were held in little cabins. In my class were Lou, a social worker in her fifties who for some reason had been assigned to the bee-keeping program; Charlie, a young blonde swimmer from Maine; and Tom, a teacher in his thirties from the Midwest. Both would work in youth development. Our instructor was a pretty *señorita* with dimples, named Sandra, who the men liked to tease. We worked on colors, time, and some conversation. I felt good at that time about my Spanish.

At home there was not lunch as Estella was busy with a birthday party for Alex. The children were scrambling in the dirt for candy spilled from a *piñata* when an ice cream wagon pulled up and dispensed strawberry cones. I had the children sing *Happy Birthday* in Spanish for me, and I then sang it in English for them.

I was happy to lie down for awhile, as the effects of the shot, my cold and the rooster's early morning call had made me weary.

At THE TRAINING CENTER each group was responsible for planting vegetables in raised beds called *huertos*. We sowed spinach, lettuce, broccoli and peppers. Of the eight of us, I was the only one with any gardening experience. Andrew was feeling so miserable I wondered if he would make it through training.

That evening I returned home to a smoky fire on the porch where Estella was making tortillas. The dried corn had been soaked in water to which lime was added and then cooked and ground into a *masa*. I took a ball of dough in my hand to try to shape it into the perfect circle, which she did so easily, but mine resembled a piece from a jigsaw puzzle!

There was good news that night. The old rooster had dropped dead of unknown causes and supper was chicken soup. Though I had grown to dislike the old bird intensely, he made good broth, but I could not bear to bite into his tough leathery leg.

During the week Mario took the group to the capital in a van to visit a typical hospital. He was both angry and embarrassed to find the doctor who had made the arrangements had forgotten we were coming. We called on the woman who was head of the nutrition for the country in the Public Health Building and Mario translated. Before we returned, he took us all to a Mexican restaurant for lunch.

Back at the center each Spanish class had its evaluation, in which Sandra rated us all "regular" which meant "so so." She informed us we were using far too much English in class and in the future must do better. This was a let-down as we thought we were doing fairly well, in addition to having a good time. I found having a non-English-speaking instructor difficult, as a question on a point of grammar which could be answered in one sentence in English often took ten minutes in Spanish.

Classes began each day at 7:30 and lasted until noon, with an hour and a half for lunch. Our day ended at 4:30.

At our first core meeting the speaker was a professor who had been a classmate of Fidel Castro. He had lived and taught in the U.S. for a period of time, admitted to being a conservative, and felt that nothing good could be achieved by violence. Besides explaining Guatemala's political parties, some of which are linked to Europe, he added that he felt United Fruit had been good for the country. He did not add that our government's meddling destroyed two good presidents who might have instigated land reform, avoiding some of the tragic problems from which Guatemala has never recovered. The political science trainees were incensed by his remarks. At that point I had not read *Bitter Fruit* and knew little of the role the United States had played.

We found we had Saturday afternoon off, and Marion and I investigated a nearby health center run by the Seventh Day Adventists. By means of a wood-stoked furnace, they maintained a spa of sorts where for a few *quetzals* (at that time four to a dollar) we could take a hot shower and a sauna followed by a massage. Lying on a table we were slapped, poked and kneaded like giant tortillas. I decided I would come again, but definitely not let the masseuse crack my neck.

On the way home we watched the misty purple clouds drop over fields of vegetables that grew high on the hills below stands of pine trees.

ESTELLA WAS LIMPING, as she had an aching hip. She needed to replace the gas tank in the kitchen, and she and Manuel Jr. struggled to get it back where it belonged. In addition, she asked to borrow ten quetzals to pay the bill. Apparently, Manuel Sr. didn't give her much money. I saw little of him, as he was a bus driver on the route from Antigua to Guate, as the capital is called. Often he left the house at 4:00, and with the rooster gone, asked to borrow my alarm clock.

In class I learned more than I ever wanted to know about worms, parasites, cysts and diarrhea. Mario had brought an ice chest his wife had packed with typical Guatemalan foods for us to sample. We were given tables of food values as well for local fruits, vegetables, and other foods that would not have been in our college dietetics charts.

Mario gave a fascinating lecture on nutritional deficiencies which we could expect to see, diseases we had only read about in college texts. The good news was that they were preventable, and we hoped, through education, we could be of help.

One morning, after nearly five hours of Spanish, I was feeling particularly depressed by my progress. Lou made me laugh on the way home by saying she usually didn't pray, but now at each meal says, "Please God, don't let me get sick from this food!"

That night about 8:00, as I was studying Spanish in my room, the lights went out. The sky was spectacular with streaked lightening, and there was nothing to do but go to bed. I awakened around 11:00, thinking a heavy door had slammed. It was a small "temblor" or earthquake and I slept poorly the rest of the night. About twenty years before, Guatemala had sustained a devastating quake which destroyed water and sewer systems and many people had died, a number from the collapse of terra cotta tile roofs.

THE SECOND WEEKEND each of us visited a successful volunteer in the field. I was paired with a young P.E. teacher from Mississippi named Bobbie. We managed to catch a bus on the highway after walking a kilometer from the training center, then hired a taxi to a bus station on the other side of town, and then boarded another bus for the site where Lisa, our hostess, would give us a glimpse of life as a volunteer.

As the bus left the highway for her town (aldea), Lisa got on carrying two chairs she had just purchased. We were glad to see her, as we were wondering how we could find her house. She lived in an attractive block house, fenced and set back in tropical shrubs and trees. There was one big room serving as a bedroom and living room, furnished with bookcases, a wooden settee, table and chairs. Her pila (tub for water) was in the kitchen, and she had a three-burner gas stove and propane tank supplied by the Peace Corps. There was even an indoor toilet and cold water shower.

Lisa was an attractive blond from California working in the forestry program. She explained she had broken her back surfing when she was in high school, and for that reason she was not allowed to use a motorcycle so had been given a site only a few hours from the capital in case of an accident. Our hostess had an early morning meeting and left Bobbie and me to have breakfast together. Bobbie turned out to be an extremely picky eater as well as a chain smoker who lived entirely on sodas and junk food. When Lisa returned, she and I fixed tuna sandwiches which Bobbie was reluctant to eat, never having eaten them before.

We visited the town's Health Care Center which had recently been vandalized and trashed. It was hard to see how this could be allowed to happen, particularly since health care was so essential.

The following day two ten-year-old neighbor girls came over and we set out for a hike to the river. On the way we met a friend of Lisa's who worked as a vaccinator for both the townspeople and their animals, in addition to raising beans and corn on her land. We walked for what seemed like miles, and I came to the conclusion I should have worn pants and hiking boots rather than a skirt and Birkenstocks. We definitely should have carried water, as the day was very warm.

Our destination was the junction of two rivers, one cold and the other running out of hot springs, which made for a wonderful two hours of swimming and soaking. Bobbie chose to sit on the bank the whole time to be bitten by flies.

On Sunday the three of us walked the four kilometers to the highway to catch a bus for the capital. Lisa took us to the Peace Corps office, and we checked in at the Spring Hotel where volunteers often stayed. Bobbie met some of her friends, and I took Lisa out to dinner. We went to an American movie, which was a good way to absorb Spanish, as nearly all films are in English with Spanish sub-titles.

My night at the Spring was a true Peace Corps experience. Lisa and I shared a room with three male volunteers. One of the men was in my training class, and if any of them thought it strange sharing a room with a sixty-two-year-old woman, nothing was said. I decided it was like being with three of my sons and went to sleep.

IN THE THIRD WEEK OF TRAINING, Mario did a demonstration on rehydration using a plastic bag full of water with a drawing of a baby on the front. By puncturing the bag, it vividly showed the effects of the loss of water by diarrhea, vomiting or crying. We had a lecture on folk medicine and some of the unusual practices used by the Mayans.

One day we spent a fascinating morning at the children's hospital for nutritional diseases. The facility was built in a park-like setting and supported by the Lion's Club of Central America. We saw bed after bed of two-year-olds the size of six-month-old babies. Generally, after a six-month stay, with proper feeding, the child could return home in good health. There were cases of both marasmus and kwashiokor—the first caused from calorie deficiency, just not enough food, and the second from insufficient protein. The tiny patients reminded me of birds that had fallen from the nest, with their huge eyes and tiny bodies. I was impressed by the loving care they received and an immaculate kitchen where food was being prepared.

EACH OF US WAS EXPECTED to present a method demonstration which we were allowed to do in English. Someone showed how to wash her hands, and I prepared an iodine solution for soaking raw vegetables. Not to be outdone, Ellen, our youngest trainee, chose to demonstrate the use of a condom using a banana.

We were all feeling homesick. Thanksgiving morning, after Spanish, we were given the option of having beans and tortillas with our families or paying for a dinner at the Ramada Hotel in Antigua. About half the group decided to go and the staff drove us to town.

We were seated at tables with starched linen cloths, flowers, candles and crystal. Dinner was a green salad with bleu cheese dressing, turkey, mashed potatoes, cauliflower and carrots, and rolls with real butter. Dessert was pumpkin pie with raisin sauce and strong black coffee. I was so keyed up from the caffeine that I had a difficult time getting to sleep that night.

At home the radio played familiar Christmas carols: *Silent Night*, *The First Noel*, and every fourth song, *Feliz Navidad*.

My family invited me to visit relatives with them in another town, but I decided, since the house would be quiet, my time would be better spent studying. I knew Estella had gone to bed around 2:00 A.M. and she was up by 6:00. I offered to dress Ingred and found she had dirty pants. Her mother took her to the pila outside and washed her from head to toe. She was a well-nourished child, but I noticed she had bites all over her body, as did I. I dressed her in a shirt, slip, yellow anklets and matching frilly dress. The family finally left in someone's truck, and it was blissfully quiet, so I was able to write my Christmas letter to be sent home, copied, and mailed in the States.

There was so much noise at my house that I stayed after school every night to study. With the money Peace Corps paid for my board and room, the family had their television set repaired, and it was placed in the boys' room next to mine. It was turned on as soon as they awakened and remained on until they went to bed. Since the time I was there was vacation for the older boys, they sometimes did nothing the entire day but watch TV. My saying, "*Margarita necessita estudiar*" meant nothing, and they saw no reason for turning down the volume. The programs seemed to be the adventures of the Flintstones and the like in Spanish.

By December the weather had changed; some days it rained hard and was cold and windy. At night unripe avocados hitting the roof sounded like falling rocks.

I had my first evaluation at the training center with the assistant Peace Corps director and another with Mario. Both were positive and encouraging.

As a group, we made our first visit to a nutrition volunteer. I was up by 5:30 in order to meet on the highway for the Guate bus. As I passed through the boys' room, they were all in one bed curled up like puppies.

Andrew threw my pack on the top of the bus, and we met Mario at a downtown market where we bought food for the next three days. I was assigned to carrying two dozen eggs in a plastic bag, which seemed like an accident waiting to happen, but fortunately did not.

Gabrielle, the volunteer, worked in a small town in cattle country, an hour and a half from the capital. The men wore cowboy boots and wide-brimmed straw hats and most carried machetes.

Christine, the health teacher in her early forties, and I shared a room in a house with a large veranda overlooking an acre of coffee trees, hibiscus and other tropical plants. The house was extremely clean and consisted of Flora, the mother, her husband, a tailor, a pretty eleven-year-old daughter and a grandson. The father had set up his treadle Singer on the porch where he was busy sewing jackets and trousers for Christmas customers.

Gabrielle was an intense young woman from New England who lived on the edge of town in a one-room adobe house with dirt floor. In one corner was a bed draped with mosquito netting. Since there was no electricity, she depended on candles for light.

Andrew and I volunteered to fix dinner the first night. Someone brought several bottles of orange wine which was consumed while we concocted a ratatoulle from eggplant, zucchini, onions, tomatoes and tomato sauce topped with grated cheese. We fixed garlic bread, and for dessert, cookies and fresh pineapple. The meal seemed to take forever to prepare in a strange kitchen by candlelight. It didn't help that Mario told me to be careful where I put my hands because of the possibility of scorpions!

In the morning we met at 7:00 to learn how to weigh and measure children. Mario drove the van about eight kilometers from town until the narrow road became too steep for safety. We walked several kilometers farther up and down hills and through streams to the school where Gabrielle had told mothers to bring their children.

Much of rural Guatemala benefits from the U.S. CARE program which distributes rice, bulgar wheat, enriched cornmeal and oil to the people. The foods were distributed through health centers, and children whose families received food were weighed and measured with records kept to assess their growth.

Fortunately, none of the mothers understood English. One woman beamed at Andrew as he lifted a small boy to the scales saying, "Up you go, you ugly little bastard."

That night, Christine, my roommate who had not felt well for several weeks, spent a miserable night with cramps and diarrhea. By morning she was so sick that Gabrielle arranged for the mayor to take her in to the nurse at the Peace Corps office. Flora, our hostess, was extremely kind and had sat by her bed holding her hand.

For our next outing it was decided I could ride on a motorcycle behind a male health worker to our destination. Wearing a helmet, I was happily buzzing up and down dusty mountain trails when someone came back and said, "Mario says Margarita is absolutely not to ride on a *moto* and to return immediately to the health center." I spent the rest of the day chatting with a young woman doctor.

Stephanie prepared dinner that night. Not only was she a registered dietitian but also proved to be a gourmet cook. We were served primavera made from thin noodles, cream sauce, crisply cooked vegetables and cheese. We were eating better on this trip than we had since arriving in Guatemala. I knew I had lost weight, as I could tuck my blouse in my skirt without a bulge showing.

One day we canvassed the town looking for children who needed to be vaccinated for polio. Each family was supposed to have an immunization record booklet. It was extremely hot, and we were attacked by small biting black flies. I had wondered why the health workers who accompanied us all wore jackets in the heat.

That evening Christine showed up feeling better. She had spent the day at the Peace Corps office and had been sent to a lab. She spent the night at the Spring Hotel, and since she had no money had to borrow from one of the nurses.

The last day we were asked to do a food demonstration at the health center. A few women came and were served spaghetti made from a soy product, bulgar salad and banana pudding. The *doctora* (doctor) had disappeared and all the men health workers left for the local bar. Flora cooked Christine and me a special dinner of chicken and rice, potatoes and vegetables. I felt she thought we looked as though we needed fattening up.

Mario had brought a VCR and television set, and we watched a tape of Guatemala, followed by a scathing satire of President Reagan. Although I was not pleased with his administration, I seemed to be the only one to find it offensive and in poor taste.

We caught a 5:00 A.M. bus for the capital and felt lucky to have seats. Christine and I spent some time Christmas shopping, and I purchased an alarm clock for Manuel Sr. and color crayons for the children.

Back home it was extremely cold. The training center was in the mountains and none of the houses had any heat. My air mattress was in Mario's car. I had my down bag but was cold the whole night, in spite of wearing pajamas, socks, sweatshirt and down vest.

The weeks before Christmas were busy. Our Peace Corps trainers gave us a day off for the week's celebration in Santa Lucia where food stalls had been set up, along with a rickety ferris wheel. Barbara and Marion and I took the bus to Antigua to do our last-minute Christmas shopping. I bought warm, red, fancy knee socks for Estella, playing cards and a book about dinosaurs and geology for the older boys, a doll for Ingred, and coloring books for the younger boys.

For Christmas dinner I ordered a cheese cake at a bakery and purchased a box of Kleenex for Barbara's present. We made reservations at the Antigua Hotel, a real luxury, for New Year's and my 30th of December birthday.

I was having trouble with Spanish. I could both read and write it better than understand it. Unlike Barbara's home, where there were three teenage girls who sat with her each night to help her with her homework, the children in my family were too small to talk much and poor Estelle felt tired and harassed much of the time. This was clearly a dysfunctional family. Manuel Sr. was seldom home, and when he was, he paid little attention to the children. On one occasion, he took the older boys to work on the farm the family owned up the mountain, but that was the only time I saw them work with their father. Estella didn't seem to require that they do any chores around the house.

The whole training group took part in a *parada* (parade). In most Latin countries there is a parade where the people symbolically look for a place for the Christ Child to be born. Men carry a small float with Mary and Joseph on top and weave their way through the streets accompanied by firecrackers, singing, castanets and drums. The idea is to go door to door asking for a place for Jesus to be born. Each house says, "No" and at the last home there is a party. In Guatemala this goes on for seven days, and on Christmas Eve, Jesus is born in the church. Generally the parada takes place at night, but our parade was held in the afternoon, and we returned to the center for hot *ponch* (punch) and tamales. Fortunately, the weather was warmer.

THIS WAS THE WEEK FOR A NUTRITION TEST. One of the girls angrily upbraided Mario over the questions, and Maria, the trainee from Mexico, flounced out after crumpling her paper and saying she hadn't studied the right things. I had managed to review the right things as I received 100.

Shortly after that, we met the doctor who would be our supervisor when we became volunteers. Sergio was a Chinese-Guatemalan pediatrician who, unlike Mario who hugged and kissed all the women, was reserved and serious. He explained in halting English the nutrition volunteer's contract with the *ministerio* of health.

One afternoon we learned how to build solar dryers from boxes and prepared beets, papaya, potatoes, pineapple, apples, and onions for drying. The only problem was that the box didn't hold much and seemed like an inefficient method for food preservation.

At that time in the United States we had four food groups, but Guatemala had only three. As there was no dairy council, the protein group included milk and milk products along with meat and beans. The protection group included fruit and vegetables, and the energy group, starches and fats.

We were each to do another method demonstration, this time in Spanish. My contribution was a song about the food groups, sung as a round to the tune of *Three Blind Mice*, which the group dutifully sang. Mario was not familiar with the tune, and my fellow trainees were not particularly impressed.

Ana, the Cuban trainee, was encouraging about my Spanish, which made me feel better after my Spanish instructor told me my problem was that I wasn't thinking in Spanish.

I don't know how Ana and Maria and a male trainee from Puerto Rico spent their time while the rest of us struggled with our Spanish, but they could have used them for tutoring those of us needing help. In addition, we were never told that behind locked doors were Spanish text books in English that could have been checked out. I had mine packed along with teaching supplies and aids to be sent via diplomatic pouch after I had completed training.

ONE SUNDAY MORNING I left with Barbara and one of the girls from her house to visit a cousin in the nearby town of Santiago. The cousin, it turned out, was related to Manuel as well.

The cousin, Melvie, met us as we got off the bus, took us to a small museum, and we walked to her house for a chat. I had hoped they would offer us something to eat as I was hungry, not having eaten my unrefrigerated tamal from last night's dinner, or my hot soybean drink. After a while Melvie stood up and said, "*Vamos*," and we headed for a market where I bought some bananas and oranges.

I looked at wool blankets, as I was tired of being cold, but both Barbara and Melvie thought sixty-five quetzals or twenty-two dollars was too much to pay, so I didn't buy any. Before we caught the bus, we found what looked like a clean restaurant where we ordered broiled meat, rolls, guacamole and coffee.

The return bus was driven by Manuel, and we asked him to let us off at the spa so that Barbara and I could treat ourselves to a hot shower.

We met Marion back at Barbara's house where I shared an anona fruit. Slightly resembling an artichoke, the inside has a creamy texture tasting like pear, pineapple and banana and is eaten with a spoon. The other women were not as impressed with it as I.

Returning home, I passed the Catholic church and joined Estella and several of the children who were sitting in the back. The sermon was on Mary's trying to find a place to have her baby. I remember his saying over and over, "Mary walked and walked."

Later, I was pleased to see Estella reading the book I had bought to the children. It was the only book in the house.

The following day we learned the Peace Corps office in Honduras had been bombed at 4:00 A.M., and as a result our office in the capital was closed for investigation. No one had picked up the mail, and the training office, as usual, had no stamps.

The whole training group took the bus to Antigua to visit a museum of musical instruments. There was an excellent slide show as well, in English, on Mayan culture.

I brought home a thick, white, woolen blanket with blue figures of women in the borders. I was pleased. After having bargained, I paid 35 quetzals or a little more than half of Sunday's price, but Estella informed me that David, the former trainee, had bought his for 25! Nonetheless, I'd be warm now. As I spread the blanket over my down bag, the children all rushed in to feel it. They all seemed to have particularly dirty hands that day.

We decorated the walls of the training center with branches of a festive red and green bromeli plant the locals called "foot of the chicken," which grows in the mountains in the upper branches of trees. The staff had hired a dance band, and I found my five-foot-eight-inch self dancing with a five-foot Spanish instructor.

Our dinner was the traditional holiday food, a tamal, and the hot fruit drink called ponch.

A nice Christmas surprise! We were all taken by bus to the Indian town of Chichicastenango, three hours away. "Chichi," as it is often called, is populated by indigenous people who wear colorful, embroidered shirts and blouses and hand-woven skirts and trousers. There are two Catholic churches built soon after the conquest, and we heard some of the twenty-six Mayan tongues.

We enjoyed pastry and coffee at a lovely hotel and browsed through open shops where I bought a white blouse with an embroidered yolk as well as some warm gloves for Marion for Christmas. In contrast, as soon as we had entered Chichi, we saw army jeeps driving through town and soldiers talking through loudspeakers. Their presence was disturbing, as that area had suffered a great deal during the war and the over-presence of the military cast a pall on everything.

I DECIDED IT WAS TIME to do some holiday cleaning, as the windows were so dirty I couldn't see out. Estella's poor, tiny, pregnant cat wanted to sleep with me, but I was having enough trouble with insect bites, without her fleas. Instead, I fed her a can of tuna.

In addition to the cat were two dogs. One was a friendly, little, pop-eyed, peke type and the other a snarly, half-grown, Doberman mix. He was chained outside my door at night, and I worried that he would sink his teeth in my ankle. I tried to impress on the boys that dogs needed water to drink, but they had a hard time remembering. During the day he was tethered out farther in the yard. Dogs seemed to be only for guarding. Never, in my whole time in Guatemala, did I see an animal being petted, talked to or loved. Cats aren't even fed, as their job is to eat rodents, snakes and birds.

David, the former trainee, had brought a Christmas tree which Estella and the boys placed in a bucket in the corner of the dining room. The crèche consisted of the Holy Family, an enormous rubber baby Jesus wearing a fuchsia-colored net dress spangled with silver sequins, and a tiny Mary and Joseph. The manger was crowded with rubber horses, cows and sheep. The boys edged the crèche with paving stones and scattered sand from the street. Surrounding all this were strings of blinding lights connected to a number of birds that chirped and whistled. The whole garish effect was overwhelming and astonishing, particularly when the little cat used the sand for her litter box.

30

The morning of Christmas Eve, Barbara and Marion and I made a trip to Antigua where Barbara bought candy for her family and I picked up the pineapple cheesecake I had ordered. We had crepes at a restaurant with an open court filled with plants.

Back home, I helped Estella with the dinner preparation. She showed me how to scoop the pulp from two pineapples after poking them with a fork, and I cut a dozen small apples for the ponch. We cut the meat of a coconut, a package of prunes, and some raisins, to which we added water to put on the fire to boil.

The tamales were made from white cornmeal, margarine, olives, capers, chicken and hot sauce. The dough (*masa*) was filled with the meat mixture and wrapped in canna lily leaves, tied, and steamed in a large pot for six hours.

While we worked, Estella talked a great deal but then burst into tears. It seemed Manuel had several other women, his bus route from Antigua to Guate making it easy to visit them. "But I am his wife," she sobbed. She told me he gave her no money, the only income being what she received from boarding trainees.

Estella's children

Estella had a head and neck ache that ran down her arm. I swept and mopped the floors and helped the boys nail branches of greens on the walls. We scattered sweet smelling pine needles over the floor and I picked some red poinsettias from across the street. Estella produced a lovely embroidered tablecloth and the room looked truly festive.

I persuaded Estella to go to bed. I left for an hour, but while I was gone Manuel Sr. had come home and they had a rousing fight. When I asked Manuel Jr. where his father was, he replied, "In the street."

At 10:00 P.M. it was time to go to mass. There was no sign of Manuel Sr., and the only children awake were three-year-old Irving and Alex. The ponch and tamals were bubbling in large pots, and we walked the three blocks to the church.

The service was by candlelight and there were song sheets with words, but I had trouble finding the right song. The whole time firecrackers exploded outside the church yard, sounding as though we were in a combat zone.

We carried home the sleeping Irving. There was no sign of Manuel Sr., and we awakened Manuel Jr. He and Alex and Estella and I shared Christmas Eve dinner. At 12:00 there were more firecrackers and we all hugged each other. Alex and his mother both cried. It was touching to see him try to comfort her.

We opened our presents. Estella had bought me a brown machine-embroidered blouse at the market. The boys were more interested in their deck of cards than the book on dinosaurs I had given them. I was sorry I had spent money on the alarm clock for their father.

Estella took the two aspirin I gave her, and we all fell into bed. And so Christmas came to this family in their poor house in Santa Lucia.

I was up before 8:00 Christmas morning. Breakfast was last night's dinner, and I shared orange marmalade that Marion had given me. Ingrid opened the package with her doll and the younger boys their color books and crayons.

My friends and I tried to attend a Protestant church in Antigua, feeling a big Lutheran church might be the most to our liking, but it was closed as their service had been Christmas Eve. We visited La Merced, a lovely old cathedral, browsed in the open tourist shops, and lunched on fruit, coffee and muffins. I received a jar of blackberry jam from Barbara. Marion was pleased with her woolen gloves and Barbara her Kleenex.

The rest of the day I spent teaching the children to play rummy and

32

crazy eights and we all colored. Manuel Sr. had returned and things seemed peaceful. He and the boys set off a huge "bomba" of gun powder packed in raffia and set in a pipe. The thought crossed my mind that it was a wonder more children didn't lose eyes and fingers.

When Marion told her family Estella was ill, they shared with her that Manuel was known for being unfaithful. He had fathered numerous children in the town up the mountain where the family had land. This was not unusual, I found out later—the faithful husband in Guatemala being the exception rather then the rule.

Shortly after the new year, our nutrition group visited a second volunteer in the field. After breakfast at McDonald's in Guatemala City, we proceeded to a bus station surrounded by a large market. We were warned to be on the watch for thieves, and I learned an important lesson.

I was wearing a straight skirt that had pockets on either side. As I was concentrating on buying vegetables, I felt a hand sliding into my pocket. I am not a screamer, but I yelled and turned at the same time and saw a man quickly leave, fortunately without my wallet. After that, I only carried loose change for bus fare in my pockets.

The six-hour bus trip to Zapatitlán near El Salvador was four hours away on paved roads and two hours on dirt, which seemed like the end of the world. Sharon was a young, pretty, brown-eyed woman from Wisconsin, engaged to a local man with a sixth-grade education.

She lived in a dirty, adobe house and was plainly not prepared for ten guests. I had brought a cooking kit with a pan, bowl, and cup, which was handy as there were few dishes. Cindy and I slept on the floor as we crowded into her three rooms. I felt sorry for Sharon when most of the group made it clear they wanted to leave the next day.

Sharon had made arrangements for each of us to visit a home to prepare a soup of Incaparina (a soy flour), water, onions and tomatoes. My house had a dirt floor and we cooked outdoors on an open fire. Wandering in and out were hens, baby chicks, and the most enormous pig I had ever seen. The grandfather came to the house and approved of the soup, which we served in tin plates with warmed-over tortillas. In the distance, we looked at the hills in El Salvador which were beautiful in the setting sun.

The next two days were spent doing demonstrations and skits. I took part in one with Cindy and Andrew that we called "The Dirty Family," who handled animals, changed the baby, cooked and picked up food without

33

washing their hands and then wondered why they got sick. We hoped that even if they could not understand our Spanish, they got the message.

Another day we walked to a school in a very poor village to give talks on vitamins and play lotteria with the women. Since the lottery is a way of life in Latin America, someone devised a game using it to teach nutrition.

The three food groups are drawn on cards, and as the different foods are called, a *lotteria* is won by having three in a row. The women enjoyed it immensely and would have been happy to have played it all afternoon. Sharon arranged for a boy to bring a live chicken (to a nearby house) which was cooked as a soup for our lunch.

Over the weekend we went for a picnic, walking four miles down to a lovely pool fed by a waterfall where we swam and lay in the sun. We caught little fresh water crabs and small fish that we cooked in a stew with tomatoes. As neither the fish nor the crabs were cleaned, I did not find the dish very *sabrosa* (tasty).

The ascent from the pool was easier than going down, but we arrived at Sharon's before dark.

The following day was stressful because Sergio, who would be our supervisor, came to interview each of us and listen to a demonstration. We tried to look our best. I lectured in my fractured Spanish on how to mix powdered milk, and even Ellen (who earlier demonstrated how to use a condom) was sufficiently subdued as she explained how to properly brush one's teeth.

We were all so glad to leave the next morning that we didn't mind getting up in time for a 3:00 A.M. bus. It was pitch black as we made our way up the hill on slippery, cobbled streets.

We were dozing when, within an hour from the capital, the bus broke down, but fortunately another soon picked us up. One more bus change, and we were back at the training center. I was delighted to have received fifteen letters when I checked my box, some of them belated Christmas cards. Next, I had a two-hour, private, Spanish lesson from the best teacher I had yet had.

Arriving home, I took a machete away from Ingred, who was playing with it in the backyard. The TV, as usual, was blaring at full volume. I seriously thought about asking for another place to stay, but with less than a month before it was time to leave, decided it wasn't worth the effort. Estella had no control over the children, and I seldom saw Manuel Sr. At

10:00 P.M. I told Manuel Jr. to turn off the television *ahorita*! Right now!

"Core" training the next day was on how to apply for grants for projects we might undertake, such as water systems or latrines. The paper work needed to be done in Spanish, and sums could be for around fifty dollars or more.

Back home, I had the usual struggle to study over the noise. Estella informed me Jaime studied very late into the night and his Spanish, unlike mine, was very good. I worked on memorizing fifty verbs useful in the kitchen.

That Saturday I left for Guate to visit friends from home who were working in the capital with "Executives Overseas," an organization using professionals to help business and industry in Third World countries. Bob and Midge were housed at the Camino Real Hotel, and Bob, a mechanical engineer, worked for a brush factory.

I had an indolent weekend of good food, access to a pool, and a beautiful room at the hotel. On Sunday, we attended a Protestant church where the service was in English. The congregation consisted of embassy people as well as some Peace Corps trainees and volunteers.

Reluctantly, I took the bus back to Santa Lucia where Marion and Barbara met me as I got off on the highway. I wondered how they knew when I was coming back.

WE WERE ASSIGNED OUR SITES to visit prior to taking final exams and "swearing in." Each of us received a folder listing the key people to contact and a description of the town. We would be traveling for a week to make introductions, arrange for housing, and introduce ourselves to our counterparts—all in Spanish. While I wasn't exactly terrified, I was apprehensive.

It was good news that Barbara was assigned to a nearby area and we could take the same buses (a total of three) to Jalapa, a fairly large town near the El Salvador border. The region was called the *oriente* (the east).

Jalapa had paved streets, stores and a big market. We met a volunteer on the street who showed us a *pensión* (hotel) where we spent the night and a restaurant where we ordered fried chicken, fries, a soft drink and a fruit cup. We paid around five dollars for our room with twin beds and a bathroom with shower and hot water. So far, so good, we thought.

Local bus

Barbara was expected to check in at the agriculture office to introduce herself. Afterwards, we found the telephone company, and I was able to get through to my youngest son and my friend Pat who was managing my affairs. She told me my house had been rented with a year's lease and everything was fine.

On the way back to our pensión, we noticed several hardware stores, a bakery, a stationery store, a drugstore and a small *supermercado*. There were few Indians. Most of the people, I was sure, were descendants of the conquistadors or mestizos, a mixture of Spanish and Indian.

We said good-bye at the bus depot. An old, square, turquoise and black bus labeled JALAPA-MONJAS-LLANO GRANDE pulled in on schedule. I waved good-bye to Barbara. I don't know when I had ever felt so alone.

From my handbag I pulled out the manila folder telling me in Spanish about Llano Grande. There were eleven hundred residents, the populace spoke Spanish, not one of the Mayan dialects, and most were farmers. The houses were adobe with tile roofs and floors of cement or earth. I would be able to stay for the week with a woman named Doña Jesus Aguirre Figueroa who was the owner of a *farmacia* (pharmacy). There were no pensiónes in town and housing was difficult to find. In addition, I read this was a tranquil town, unlike Monjas, nine kilometers away, known for its violence. For that reason, there had not been volunteers in the area.

The bus took me through the city of Jalapa, past a large army base. The hills were dry with a few sparse trees and rocky outcroppings. Every so often we passed houses. This was the dry season and I saw no evidence of farming. Eventually, we descended to a river where women were washing clothes and naked children played in the water. We crossed a bridge covered with wooden planks that clattered under the weight of the bus.

The road took us through a rather attractive town, which I judged to be the violent Monjas. A number of passengers got off and more got on, carrying vegetables and other goods in baskets. After three or four miles, we left the highway onto an unpaved road. We curved between plowed fields lined on one side by brick and adobe houses. Eventually, we reached an irrigation canal and fields of tomatoes, peppers, onions, and broccoli. Crossing the canal, we started up the mile to Llano Grande.

I told the driver I was looking for the farmacia, and he pointed up the street. Aware that everyone was studying me intently, it reminded me of my arrival forty years before at a little town in the Palouse hills of eastern Washington, where I was a new teacher. The street was steep, dusty, unpaved, and studded with rocks. I saw a church that said in Spanish, *Mont*

Llano Grande where Marge lived.

of Olives Evangelical, and on the other side, the pharmacy.

As I entered the door, a pleasant woman about my age greeted me. Suddenly, I could not remember a word of Spanish, and she tactfully suggested I sit on the bench to regain my composure.

The drugstore had an amazing assortment of goods. It smelled of medicine, soap, and dust. There were boxes of pills, salves, ointments, toothpaste, baby cologne and powder. On shelves were rubber dolls, school supplies, groceries, bananas, and tomatoes. The pharmacy also served as a center, as it contained the post office and the only telephone in town, although I found out later, as a line was down, it was non-functional. Doña Chusita, the feminine nickname for Jesus, as my folder told me, was a town leader, owned the pharmacy, was postmistress and a nurse.

When I could talk, I told her I was Margarita from Cuerpo de Paz, as Peace Corps is called in Spanish. She immediately asked my church affiliation, and I told her I was Methodist, but not evangelical. This seemed to be acceptable to her as long as I was Protestant, for whenever she introduced me it was, "This is Margarita. She is Protestant but not evangelical." Apparently, I had passed the first test.

THE PHARMACY WITH ITS ADJOINING BUILDINGS covered perhaps half of a city block. The walls were topped with cemented shards of glass, for protection, enclosing a patio surrounded by connecting rooms. On one side was a covered porch with hanging ferns and other luxuriant plants. Chusita showed me to a room directly behind the pharmacy. Next was a large, screened, dining room and kitchen with a four-burner gas stove. Beyond was a large guest bedroom; on the other side, another bedroom, and then a covered traditional kitchen with a clay oven and adobe stove. I saw two pilas, one outside the kitchen and another in front of the shower room. There was a toilet with a seat, which was unique, although there was seldom enough water for flushing.

Beyond the compound was a garden space tangled with weeds, orange trees, limes, several papayas, bananas, guavas, and pomegranates. There was a large, fenced, chicken coop, holding ducks and turkeys as well.

The household at that point consisted of Chusita, who told me she had had eight children, six of whom lived in the capital. An older son, Jaimie, lived near Washington D.C., where he worked in construction, and there was a son "in heaven." Her husband, Moses, worked as a sanitarian at a health center near Puerto Barrios far away on the Caribbean. She herself had visited in the United States several times.

Moses' mother lived in the house also and helped in the store. She reminded me of a frail little bird.

Alicia was a delightful young woman in her late twenties who did some of the cooking, but her primary job was as a religious education director for the church.

The last person I met was Jorge, pronounced "Horhay," who told me he had worked in South America, Pennsylvania and Spain. He seemed to be affiliated with the church but was also some sort of dental technician. Jorge was a big, friendly man with graying curly hair who was nice enough to compliment me on my Spanish.

For lunch Alicia prepared small fish cooked with tomatoes and peppers over rice. One of my fish had a piece of tomato in its mouth and I told them the dish was *muy elegante*.

Linda in front of the health center

After lunch, I met the mayor to tell him I planned to live in Llano Grande for two years to work in the health center, teach health and nutrition in the schools, encourage vegetable gardens, and if possible get some latrines built.

I walked to the health center called a *puesto de salud* (health post). On the porch wall was a plaque stating it had been built by Canadian CARE. The puesto was closed, as government employees were on vacation.

Next door was a small

tienda (store), selling cold drinks, cigarettes, rice, beans, beer and sugar. Coming out to greet me was Linda, the nurse who was to be my counterpart. Linda was small, in her early twenties with dark hair pulled back in a long braid. She was extremely friendly and had hazel eyes, which was unusual for a Guatemalan, and though not beautiful, was attractive. I liked her immediately and felt we could both work together and be friends. Most important, we were able to communicate. She told me when she had a long distance to go to make calls she sometimes rode a horse and would be able to get one for me. The last time I had ridden was in the wheat fields in Pullman, Washington, forty years before when I was in college, and that was a disaster. I would have to think about that, I decided.

There was an acute water shortage in town. Linda assured me there were seeds in the yard around the puesto and when the rains came everything would be green and flowering. She had planted mangoes and other trees and she and her husband lived in a room in the back of the health center, cooking and eating behind the tienda.

I read before I went to sleep. There was electricity, meaning I could use my curling iron and plug in a student lamp for better light. I was grateful to be alone, as the stress of meeting so many new people and communicating totally in Spanish was tiring, but I felt I had perhaps jumped an important hurdle.

After a breakfast of bananas, cornflakes and hot milk, I explored the other end of town toward the school. I passed the Catholic church, which seemed to be in the process of renovation, and adobe houses set back in fenced yards. There was not a paved street in town. A few tropical trees gave some shade, and most homes showed some attempt to plant colorful bougainvilleas or hibiscus. A turkey hen herded her poults down the road. I wondered how their owners sorted them out. Dogs were so thin I could count their ribs. Since this was obviously horse and cow country, I needed to watch where I stepped.

Emaciated dog

Garbage, apparently, was simply swept out the door, as papers, plastic bags and straws littered both sides of the street.

The school was located about three blocks from my house. Constructed of concrete blocks and built in an L shape, it had tile floors and covered porches. The principal introduced herself as Aida and seemed pleased when I told her I would like to teach health and nutrition to the children. She asked for an outline of what I planned to teach and thought the idea of a school garden was a good plan. I left, as she was busy registering children, and felt good about our visit.

Maria, the 4-H leader, lived in a large house across from the health center. There was a veranda with hammocks and benches built around the living quarters. I explained I was a home economics teacher and hoped she would let me help out at some of her meetings. She told me on Mondays and Fridays she had as many as fifty-five señoritas and married women come there to do crafts, sew and cook.

The following day Chusita and Jorge took me by truck to visit the mayor in the next town, Monjas. I was a little embarrassed by my appearance. Wearing a longish cotton skirt and, because it was cold, a sweat shirt and anklets with my Birkenstock sandals, I was hardly a picture of fashion. The truck windows had been rolled down and my hair did not look its best. I decided to neither apologize for my appearance nor my Spanish and held out my hand to introduce myself.

The mayor was a sophisticated young man wearing designer jeans and a star of David on a chain around his neck. He said he had lived in Los Angeles and agreed that there was serious malnutrition and poverty in the area. My audience over, I joined Chusita who had been shopping. Jorge drove us home.

Even though Canadian CARE constructed a water system for the town, there was not adequate water for their needs. Linda told me she knew a place where we could bathe. The weather had turned a little warmer, and we walked a kilometer through fields and over stone walls to a pretty, wooded place where water came from a pipe forming a knee-deep pool. I asked Linda if there were snakes and she replied, "Only in the wet season." In Guatemalan fashion, we striped to our underwear and both washed our long hair. The water was a trifle chilly, but it felt good to be clean. At Chusita's there was only enough water for cooking and drinking.

That night both Alicia and Chusita asked me to attend church. Psalms were sung from the Bible which was, I imagined, how they were meant to be sung. I was introduced to the congregation and asked if I were contented in Guatemala and which church I represented from home. The midweek service lasted two hours.

The following morning I paid Chusita for my room and board, and she said I would be able to live with them at the farmacia. My rent would be eight dollars a month. Although this was not the housing I had envisioned, my own house with a hammock on the porch and space for a garden, there seemed to be no other place to stay. However, I was being sent to this site because there was a need for a volunteer and everyone made me feel most welcome. The family was educated, could help me with Spanish, and I would certainly be safer than if I lived alone.

I was up by 5:00 for the 6:00 A.M. bus. The bus helper, a cheerful, friendly, young man, greeted me with enthusiasm as he took my backpack and said, "*Margarita, mi amiga.*"

In the capital I headed for the Camino Real Hotel and met Midge McRae who was just leaving the dining room. She had worried about me all week, knowing how uneasy I was. Over fried shrimp, beer and a chocolate sundae (I was actually trying to gain weight), I told her about my week. It was nice to have someone concerned about me, and I soaked in her bathtub and then watched the inauguration of President Bush on CNN television.

MARIO INVITED THE TRAINING GROUP to a picnic in the country at a finca owned by someone in his family. It was a beautiful place set in an orchard of peaches, plums and apples in full bloom. Sergio and his Chinese wife and two small boys were there as well as Lily, Mario's wife, and son. The women served wine, *ceviche* (vegetables), grilled beef, Spanish rice and green salad. Some of the other groups had done more socializing with their instructors, but I appreciated their hospitality. I was sorry I hadn't tried to communicate with Sergio's wife after I learned she had been educated in China in English schools.

Several of us walked into a town that had a telegraph office before we caught the bus. I was able to reach my daughter-in-law in Danbury, Connecticut, for the first time. My son Steve had left for a physics teachers' conference in San Francisco, but I told them to bring the children and visit me in August.

With only two weeks until our swearing in, the fear of failing Spanish exams loomed over my head. We were all feeling pressured and unsure of ourselves. It was clear at least four of the older trainees would be sent home.

Our biggest assignment was to put on *"El Dia del Campo"* (field day for the families hosting trainees). This meant providing lunch for around three hundred people, planning activities and giving out awards. The nutrition group was assigned to be in charge of the food, a huge headache none of us needed.

The day before the celebration, Estella, who had tried to get one hundred ripe avocados at fifteen centavos each, told me the deal had fallen through. I was in charge of making twelve batches of unbaked oatmeal cookies made from margarine, sugar, cocoa and vanilla, which were heated and poured over oatmeal and then rolled into balls. Fortunately, I had lots of help. The very overweight head of the Spanish Department asked if she could sample a few crumbs, and then she consumed at least a pound of cookies, but one did not deny her anything the week before finals!

The 4-H trainees slaughtered twenty chickens they had raised. The poor things were hung by their feet on a line before their throats were cut. Not having lived on a farm, I was unnerved. The chickens were parboiled with rice and the vegetables we had grown.

El Dia del Campo was a success. Stephanie, a dietitian, and some of the other trainees had done most of the shopping in the capital. The affair pulled the training group together in a cooperative team. It was too bad we couldn't have done it earlier before we were so pressured. I helped make guacamole. There were huge vats of cabbage slaw, green salad, the chicken, which miraculously did not spoil overnight, punch, cookies and fruit. We decided to add hot dogs and found the wieners the size of my finger and individually wrapped in plastic, which took longer to prepare than we had planned. In addition, the buns were so stale we had to steam them to soften.

The "mothers" of the trainees and some of the fathers and myriads of children descended on us. The Youth Development group had stations where games such as poster painting, water-filled balloon toss and races took place. One of the men in beekeeping drew a crowd by putting a queen bee on his chin and growing a beard of bees. Certificates were given out and each mother received a long-stemmed red rose.

We had grown much of the food for *El Dia del Campo*, but the balance we paid for. I was disappointed to see many of the families going through the food line more than once in order to take food home.

I was doing my studying at the training center after school or at Barbara's house where it was quiet. She and I made a trip to Antigua where I haggled at the market over a cotton rug in shades of blue, pink and lavender. At a book store I found a print of the corn harvest to match the rug. The painting was symbolic of the belief held by the Mayans that the sun god provided the corn which sustained them, and after death, as a reward, their bodies nourished the maize. I had two decorations for my nine-by-eleven-foot room in Llano Grande.

Our technical training talk was on weaning and breast feeding. I did a talk on the way our bodies use iron by drawing construction men carrying iron which represented red blood cells. To complete the process the body needs vitamin C. Mario was pleased.

One Sunday I studied at Marion's house. She had bought a birthday cake for one of the children and invited me to dinner. We had chicken and rice, a vegetable salad and hot chocolate. I was envious of her clean house, with the bonus of no television.

In the last several weeks we had six-hour Spanish classes. I didn't feel good about my progress, was angry about my living conditions, and wished the trainers were not so emphatic about the possibility of our failing.

We had sessions with the head of the Peace Corps business office telling us about our salaries. We received a little over two hundred dollars in quetzals, which was the equivalent to the salary of a nurse or teacher. There was as well a sum for "settling in," money used for dishes, utensils and furniture. Monthly checks were deposited in a city bank, and we could draw money by check from a local bank.

Things suddenly began to look up. I had the first part of my Spanish test with a cheerful positive woman who had come from the capital, and I was feeling better as I returned to my dirty house where, much to my surprise, the TV was off.

On the last week of Spanish we had several days of individual tutoring. One was a practice session with Elsa, the supervisor, and a male instructor. Pretending to be the mother of eight children, all of whom had diarrhea, he asked me what to do. I told him to make a drink of boiled water, lemon

44

juice, sugar, a pinch of salt, and a little baking soda and to visit the nurse at the health center. I added it might be a good idea to discuss family planning with her as well, which both thought terribly funny.

On the last day we attended a class on first aid given by a volunteer in the nursing program, and around 5:00 P.M. I was informed I had passed and would be a volunteer. We celebrated by going to a café on the highway for hamburgers, fries and hot chocolate. Our friend, Lou, whose Spanish was good, had not passed in the beekeeping program. She was told she could appeal in Washington, but it would be an expensive process with no guarantee of success. She would have made a good volunteer, and we all wrote letters to Peace Corps explaining why she should continue.

Back home, two-year-old Ingred had the flu, Manuel Sr. who had had a cold the last few weeks was still snuffling, Estella had a sinus headache, and the boys were arguing and crying.

For some reason all the children washed that night. There were times their hands were so dirty that before dinner I took all five of them to the pila to wash their hands with my soap. Best of all, the TV was still off. The reason, I found, was that it was broken.

The final day of classes Mario lectured on feeding severely malnourished children. If given too much food too rapidly, it is possible to overload their digestive systems, causing death.

I told Mario I had an invitation from a couple I had met from U.S.A.I.D. to go to El Salvador, and he told me I absolutely could not go. An American citizen could be kidnapped, he said, and held for ransom.

As part of the final festivities there was a pizza party and talent show, but I had made an appointment for a permanent at a tienda on the corner. The result was shorter bangs than I wanted, but it would be easier to care for. I'd never before had my hair rinsed in a pila.

Feeling guilty about my feelings toward the family, I suggested to Estella we take the children to a playground in Antigua for the afternoon. For three hours they played on swings, slides, ropes and a jungle gym. I bought ice cream cones and we brought home a watermelon for dinner.

ON THE LAST DAY our "swearing in" took place at the training center. It was also the first day of school. The children were not out of bed early enough, and there was a great deal of noise and

45

squabbling. No one ever seemed to leave in time.

We were told to bring one dressy dress and "fashionable shoes" for the women and sport coat, shirt and tie for the men. Wearing a pleated, voile, East Indian dress and sandals, I sat with my group in the meeting room. There was an American flag and a Guatemalan flag. The American ambassador, Peace Corps director, and training director all addressed us in Spanish. Ana, the Cuban/American woman from our group, had been chosen to give the response. We raised our right hands and swore to uphold the constitution of the United States. Forty-six of the original fifty-seven of us were now Peace Corps volunteers. The attrition had occurred for a number of reasons. Some had not met the standards for technical training or Spanish. However, most chose to return to the United States, due to having suffered from culture shock, homesickness or illness. One young man had stayed only three days.

The then U.S. ambassador, whom we suspected would have preferred to have nothing to do with the Peace Corps, left as soon as possible with six armed bodyguards in two cars with flashing lights.

We were served a catered lunch on the porch. A cold wind blew down on us from the hills.

February 1989

I finished packing, kissed Estella and the children good-bye, and put on a clean blouse. Estella began to cry. By then I had seven pieces of luggage, including a box of teaching materials which we managed to carry to Barbara's house where the Peace Corps truck would pick them up to be stored at the office in Guate. As I walked by the corner where my family lived, they were all standing in the street and Estella was still crying. I felt guilty because I was so happy to leave.

BARBARA, MARION, AND I shared a room at a downtown hotel in the capital. Since they both felt as though they were coming down with the flu, they were happy to go to bed, while I had a farewell dinner with Midge and Bob at their hotel.

We were up early for an embassy briefing. Embassy guards thoroughly searched my camera bag and deposited it on a shelf. We were given maps of Guatemala with high-lighted areas considered unsafe because of drug trafficking or guerrilla activity. Most interesting was a card with code phrases to use in case of trouble.

Our first experience with Spanish banking went well. The first month's checks had been deposited at a downtown bank, and we successfully withdrew the money.

Again, we had a sleepless night. Both women were worse and coughed most of the time.

THE RAIN CAME DOWN IN SHEETS as we headed for the Peace Corps office by taxi to collect our belongings. Barbara checked in with the nurse who found she had a temperature of 104. I told her I had shared a bed with Barbara for the last two nights and asked if she could give me anything in case I came down with whatever she had, but I was snippily informed that since I wasn't sick I certainly couldn't have any medication.

Since Bobbie and Ana were going to Jalapa, we piled our luggage into two taxies and found the bus station. The ride there took over three hours, and the women left me waiting for the Llano Grande bus surrounded by my heap of luggage.

I had a three-hour wait in Jalapa and bought a couple of baskets, some oranges and a pineapple. Sitting on the curb, I signed some valentines for my grandchildren and wrote postcards. The ice cream man and his friend peered over my shoulder and picked out the word "embassy" on the post card I was writing.

On every bus is an *ayudante* (a helper) who collects fares, but only after the bus is underway, stepping over and around passengers standing in the aisles. He helps mothers on with babies, baskets, and chickens, and loads large items on top. When he wants people to move back, he calls out, "*Dele dele dele!*" (Give it). One of his jobs is leaning out the door to let the driver know when it is safe to pass on a curve.

Chema was the name of our ayudante. He recognized me and cheerfully loaded my two-years' worth of gear on the top for the hour-and-a-half ride to Llano Grande.

It was dark when we arrived and people carried my belongings to the pharmacy. I made my bed, did a little unpacking, and was grateful Chusita gave me dinner, after which I was happy to go to bed.

I spent the morning unpacking and sorting my clothes, books and teaching materials. Chusita suggested I have floor-to-ceiling shelves built by a carpenter. In the meantime she brought me a bench for my things. I would have put blouses and dresses on hangers but needed to buy concrete nails to pound in the wall. My room was windowless. Three sides were new brick. The wall behind my bed could be best described as puce colored and had a floor-to-ceiling crack. It was furnished with a narrow metal bed, wooden table, a very hard chair, a bedside table and a lamp. A support

My room is 9 x 11. This chair is incredibly hard.
Photos of friends and family above desk.

beam ran under the red-tiled roof and the floor was concrete. The door opened onto a patio complete with wooden settee, some chairs and a coffee table. Chusita had a green thumb, and ferns and other potted plants were luxurious and lush.

I was invited to a meeting at the health center that afternoon, where I was introduced along with Sarita, the new doctora, to several midwives and to a number of health promoters. With my limited Spanish, much went over my head.

That evening I fixed packaged soup and went to bed early in order to be up at 5:00 for shopping and banking in Jalapa the next day.

I CAUGHT THE BUS for Jalapa by my house at 6:00 A.M. The road was unpaved and the vehicle swayed, coughed and bumped as it made its way to the highway. The sky was beginning to turn pink as sleepy passengers appeared from the darkness. Chema helped small children up the steps, placed boxes and large items on top, jumping aboard as the bus rolled down the dusty road. I saw scrawny cows being milked and a wife scattering corn for the chickens.

Nursing babies nuzzled their mother's plump breasts and toddlers pressed button noses against dusty windows as the helper collected fares and handed out tickets. Rosy streaks in the sky turned to blue as the sun appeared above ridges of pines on the hills. It took half an hour before we reached the highway for the hour's ride to Jalapa on pavement.

Walking to the telephone company, I tried without success to call one of my sons. I was just finishing my pancakes in the nearby hotel when a young man appeared saying, "Hello, you must be one of the new volunteers." He introduced himself as Don Billett and said he lived in the mountains on a finca and came in every weekend to see his Guatemalan girlfriend.

Don explained that he worked in animal husbandry and needed to buy vaccines, but he would like to show me the city and some stores where I might shop. We went to the bank and the open market, and he pointed out several grocery stores. He also helped me buy cement nails, as both words were beyond my vocabulary. Later we met for lunch at the Oriental Chicken restaurant where he introduced me to several other volunteers.

While waiting for my 4:30 bus, I was pleased with my shopping effort. I had purchased yarn; staples such as tuna, mayonnaise, peanut butter, and coffee; fresh fruits and vegetables along with a bag to carry them; and a wicker basket for my mail. It was dark when I returned. On the way up to Llano Grande, we waited half an hour for a broccoli truck to load, as the road was too narrow for the bus to pass.

It was nice to be able to prepare my own food. My dinner consisted of an avocado stuffed with tuna salad, sliced cucumbers, fresh pineapple and lemonade. The bad news was that I was coming down with Marion's and Barbara's cold.

On my first Sunday the sun came out and I hoped my solar shower would heat sufficiently for a hot shower. The cold had settled in my throat, and I croaked as I attempted Spanish. I attended church but went with Alicia to her Sunday School department. The children were well behaved and interested. Alicia had a loving and gentle way with them as she told stories and taught them songs and Bible verses. The total service was two hours. Selfishly, I was there to listen to Spanish, although in order to be part of the community I had decided to attend church when I was in town on Sunday.

50

That afternoon I did my washing, used my new shower, and lay in the hammock translating from a book called *Helping Health Workers Learn*.

Starting my first week as a volunteer, I was up by 6:30 to find customers in the farmacia buying sweet rolls, pencils and notebooks, or medicine. I ate my breakfast in the *comedor* (dining room) where various members of the family gathered. Alicia did some of the cooking, but I was on my own, which worked out well for me. I had access to the refrigerator in the store which was filled with soda pop, over-the-counter drugs, food, and frozen popsicles. A large poster fastened to the refrigerator proclaimed in Spanish, "Jesus Is Coming. Are You Ready?"

Promptly at 8:30 I arrived at the health center to find Linda inexplicably gone for the week. I chatted with Sarita, the doctora who told me her home was in Monjas and she would commute daily. She would like to learn English, especially since her brother-in-law was from Florida. Her sister had been a music major and married an American engineer. They had just recently visited and she had not been able to communicate.

Sarita was tiny, had a beautiful smile, dimples, and a warm friendly manner. I'm sure she didn't lack for beaus among her classmates. When the first patient arrived, I left.

Classroom

51

My afternoon was spent at a 4-H meeting. Maria, the leader, was a delightful woman in her forties. She had several sons attending agricultural college, a teenage girl at home and a younger boy. We met on her veranda which was lined with benches and chairs. I was surprised to see forty girls and young women crocheting and embroidering. A few babies were crawling on the tile floor or held by a young mother or older sister. I had brought my knitting and the girls gathered around to inspect it. Later, Maria and the girls prepared chicken and rice with sauce.

I felt better the next day but had a sore throat. I decided it would be good for my Spanish to attend school and sit in on classes for a couple of weeks. Aida, the principal, welcomed me warmly, and I spent two hours with her six- to eight-year-olds. During recess we talked about the possibility of planting school gardens on the grounds. She thought I would need to provide fencing.

Back home, the solar shower was so hot I needed to add cold water in order to wash my hair. I had a box of teaching materials to sort through, posters to color, and a health book in Spanish called *Between Mother and Child*.

On my shortwave radio, I was only able to get Cuba and Taiwan and was feeling so bad I went to bed again at 8:00. I found I had a temperature of over 100 and was sick all the next day, accomplishing only studying verbs and reading teaching materials.

Awakening in the middle of the night, my fever was down but I was left with a croupy cough. The morning was spent in the sixth-grade class listening to a no-nonsense male teacher teach about Roman numerals. I wondered how useful this would be to any of the students.

I had arranged to meet Barbara in Jalapa where she was attending a 4-H meeting. The only room she could get at the hotel was upstairs in the old part, a depressing place with exposed wiring and a single light bulb hanging from the ceiling. I went to bed while Barbara went out to buy me some cough medicine. Even with that, we both coughed most of the night. Twice I awakened to hear rats scurrying around above us and in the walls.

It took an hour and a half to set up our checking accounts. At the door were two armed guards, which we were not sure should make us feel safer or that we were at immediate risk of an armed robbery. The teller said our money should be there by the next Wednesday.

WALKING THROUGH THE MARKET, which covered a city block, we saw tables of produce—pineapples, bananas, apples, cantaloupe, little sweet watermelons, cucumbers, carrots, potatoes and broccoli. Some stalls had ribbons, buttons and sewing supplies. There was cheese, white and crumbly, fried tortillas, blocks of raw sugar covered with flies, and tables of fresh flowers such as gladiolus, chrysanthemums, statice and baby's breath. Outside, vendors sold live chickens, ceramic pots and kindling. One section displayed leather goods, such as saddles and horse supplies; another, shoes and clothing; yet another baskets and hammocks. I could buy a machete, groceries, batteries and meat all under one roof.

We ate fruit for lunch, and I tried to sleep while Barbara went to the telephone company in an attempt to call her daughter in Louisiana.

When I took the early bus back to my village the next morning, I had the worst case of bronchitis I had ever had. I was tired from lack of sleep but lying down made the coughing worse.

Sunday I attended church. The minister, accompanied by a young man on a guitar, played the music on a small accordion. I got little out of the sermon, which seemed to be more of a discussion. Pablo, the minister, invited me to go for a walk after church with his family and back to their

Llano Grande

53

home for dinner. Eloisa and Pablo, I would guess, were in their early thirties. The children were Carolina, a thin nine-year-old; Abner, eight; Pablo Jr., five; and three-year-old Otto, pronounced "Oh-to."

We walked past the school and turned on a dusty road that wound up a steep hill. Climbing higher on goat paths through dry grass, cactus and century plants we could look down on the village. On one side was a river bordered by pines and tropical trees; on the other a flat plain or *llano*, and in the distance cone-shaped volcanoes. Beyond, they told me, was the *frontera* of El Salvador. Pablo had climbed some of the volcanoes when he was younger. Both he and his wife grew up in a city thirty kilometers away. Carolina was adopted and had been with them since infancy, and the boys were handsome and looked well cared for.

Back at the parsonage, which adjoined the church, we had supper on the veranda. Eloisa prepared black beans, tortillas, broccoli and tomato salad. In the traditional kitchen was an adobe stove in addition to a gas plate. Their pila was outside the kitchen, adjacent to a well where they hauled water in a bucket with a rope and pulley. My hostess said they had been exposed to American cooking through missionaries with whom they had worked, and she would like to learn more, as well as how to bake

Linda on a horse.

bread.

By Monday Linda was back at the clinic. My cough sounded so bad that Sarita listened to my chest, determined I didn't have pneumonia, and gave me more cough syrup.

I spent the morning studying records of children who had been seen at the clinic to determine which ones were malnourished. A red dot designated the most severely malnourished (*desnutrido*) who could die; yellow, children at risk; and green for healthy. Interestingly, these colors were appropriate for Guatemala in that the Mayan color for death is red, and the sign of a healthy harvest is green. I got some idea of the towns and hamlets served by the puesto. Linda was still talking about making rounds on horseback.

I was sitting in the back of the third-grade classroom coughing when a young gringo came in. He introduced himself as Buck and said Sergio suggested he look me up and we get together to pool our talents. Buck was from New England, graduated from Harvard, and planned to apply for medical school when he finished Peace Corps. We were both to attend a meeting at the hospital in Jalapa where he was making a presentation.

The following day in Jalapa was frustrating. Barbara's and my checks had not cleared. I was able to cash a fifty dollar traveler's check, but Barbara, who had taken a 3:00 A.M. bus, was able to get the bank manager to change only twenty dollars. He would not take one of her bills, for he said it looked "too new."

The meeting at the hospital was attended by Sergio, a Dr. Polonky of the Ministerio of Health, two gringos working for CARE, and me. Buck presented a request for a health program in his village he was asking CARE to finance. I understood little other than that, and I never found out if he was successful. After four hours, I excused myself and caught a bus for the capital.

FOR TWO NIGHTS I STAYED WITH MARION, who was renting the upper floor of a new house on the outskirts of a town called Ciudad Vieja that had been the original capital before a giant mud slide wiped out everything. It was cold and windy and we spent our time going over ideas for teaching foods and nutrition. Her job in 4-H was to work with girls placed in group homes and children in an orphanage nearby.

In Guatemala City I saw Midge and Bob, who were still working for Executives Oversees. I soaked in their bathtub for an hour, and they supplied me with more cough medicine and fed me lunch.

I spent the next night with a friend from home and her daughter who had left the Peace Corps just before I came. Kathy had developed an extremely successful knitting project in the town where our training group had visited Sharon. The women not only learned knitting but also marketing and purchasing skills as well. One twelve-year-old girl earned enough money for her family to build a new adobe house. The sweaters were sold in California.

In Jalapa, there was a big line of people waiting for the Llano Grande bus, but the crowd made sure I was pushed on and a couple had me sit between them.

AT THE SCHOOL BOTH STUDENTS and teachers did janitor work—sweeping, washing windows, watering plants and cleaning blackboards. The women teachers were all very friendly, but the male sixth-grade teacher was a sourpuss—in Spanish *cara de vinagre* (face of vinegar).

Never did I see him smile, although he had control of his class and I was inclined to think him a good teacher.

At home Chusita was giving Dobie, the dog, cough medicine. She said everyone was coughing because of the dust. Dobie had decided the rug by my bed was a good place to sleep, but I told him, "*Vaya*" (You go).

I found I was eating things I seldom did at home, such as Tang, Jell-O, and chocolate pudding. I had lost fifteen pounds, partly from a change in diet, the heat, and a great deal of walking. I was obviously not getting much fat.

Talk at the health center

ONE AFTERNOON WE PLAYED NUTRITION LOT-
TERY at the health center. There were ten patients, three children, Sarita,
Linda, and a health promoter who dispensed birth control information.
That day I did my first talk on nutrition. I wondered how much my audi-
ence got from my charla, but I had begun!

Linda asked me to go to Jalapa with her. Stopping at the bank, my
check had come back *sucia* (dirty). In my attempt to write my first check
in Spanish, I had inadvertently reversed the amount and payee. As I carefully wrote out a new check, I thought to myself that American banks were
more forgiving and wondered what would happen should I ever overdraw
my account!

While Linda shopped for goods for her tienda, I stopped at a stationery
store to buy a three-ring punch called a *perfordora*, masking tape called
just plain tape, and marking pens which were *marcadoras*.

AT 4-H THERE WERE THIRTY SEÑORITAS, and I
taped up charts I had made identifying the three food groups. Maria's husband happened to be home and volunteered to call the names of the different foods from slips of cardboard for lotteria. My nutrition talk, I thought,
was a little more understandable, and Maria told me she was delighted to
have help with her meetings. She added that she was sending me a chicken.

True to her word, Jeanette, her teenage daughter, arrived the next day
with a live chicken tucked under her arm. For a moment I was at a loss for
words. I know they thought I was a wimp when I said I had never killed a
chicken. She laughed and took it home, but the next day I found it in a
plastic bag in the refrigerator complete with feet, head, and beak. I later
found I could buy frozen chicken in Jalapa—cleaned, plucked and without the feet.

One Sunday Linda asked me to visit friends with her who lived up in
the hills. We walked toward the area where we had showered the month
before, up through dry stream beds, fields, and woodlands until we reached
a small town called La Cruz. Continuing climbing, we crawled over boulders and walked up a narrow trail. Crossing the stream, we climbed an
even steeper area where we were joined by an old man. The three of us

Village people and women's group

shared popsicles Linda had managed to keep frozen by storing them in a container used for vaccines.

The friends' house was a large, whitewashed, adobe structure with a wide veranda containing benches and seats. Our hostess, who was seven months pregnant with her twelfth child, greeted us warmly. There were eleven children from three to twenty-three, all of whom were clean and reasonably well dressed, and the amazing thing was that they all were still living at home.

We were served tortillas with honey, sweetened coffee and scrambled eggs. The husband came in from the fields with one of his sons who carried a large black duck. In the dirt courtyard outside the veranda were several horses, some pigs, a family of dogs and a cat.

Water was obtained from a small stream, and the toilet seemed to be anywhere in the sugar-cane field. There was no electricity.

The kitten loved sitting on my lap. I doubt if anyone had ever held or petted her.

I rather hoped we wouldn't stay to eat the black duck, but several hours later I was handed a plate of rice covered with slices of duck in a sauce and more sweetened coffee. The table was so small we ate in shifts.

When it was time to leave, seven of the children accompanied us down the mountain. The family must have been fairly affluent as some of the girls had gold work in their teeth. They chatted with us for a kilometer or so, helping me over waist-high boulders which blocked the stream bed.

Linda said she knew a shortcut home, and we scrambled through underbrush for what seemed like hours. We found an orange tree with ripe fruit, but the oranges were sour like lemons. It was nearly dark when we finally reached the tienda that Linda and her husband, Alfonso, built next to the health center. I collapsed in their hammock and downed two bottles of ice-cold Coke, called *Cocas*, another thing I generally didn't drink at home but was so dehydrated I needed it.

When I arrived at the puesto the next morning at 8:00, the room was full of patients. No one seemed in need of urgent care, for when I suggested they might like to hear about the three food groups and play lotteria, everyone took part, including Sarita and Linda.

I left for school and sat in on a history lesson comparing the Mayans with the Egyptians. That afternoon, for reasons not explained to me, the puesto was closed, and I was able to spend my time studying Spanish and coloring charts.

The sky was cloudy and the air seemed cool but not cold. I was puzzled by the black grit that seemed to be collecting on every flat surface. Chusita explained it was *arena* from the volcano Pacaya. My dictionary said *arena* was sand, which this resembled, but was nothing like the fluffy gray material we experienced six years before when Mount St. Helen's erupted. I swept out at least a cupful from my room twice a day. Tile roofs, I found, are neither totally water nor sand nor bug proof.

ARMED WITH A LARGE PLASTIC JUG of lice remedy, Linda, Sarita and I headed for a neighboring aldea. We walked a mile up a hill, descending upon a lovely river shaded with trees. We crossed, stepping on large flat rocks to the other side, and walked a trail through pines and tropical trees I didn't recognize to a large field until we came to a dirt road. This was Rinconada. There was no running water, electricity or latrines. Though a more attractive site than Llano Grande, everything seemed poorer. Children were dirtier, clothes more shabby, and in general the people more unhealthy.

Linda and Sarita handed out packets of oral rehydration remedy used for diarrhea and checked family records of immunizations. Some families were afraid to have their children vaccinated, and these were the ones who contracted polio and measles.

Here we visited the home of a terribly malnourished three-month-old whose mother, Linda explained, was loco and refused to feed the child. Sarita told the grandmother to feed the baby the soy preparation, Incaparina, mixed with water.

At home I swept more black sand from my room. It was cold enough to spread my down bag over my wool blanket, and in the morning I put on both a sweater and a down vest. Although it was windy, the ash seemed to have stopped raining down on us.

Maria was lying down when I dropped by to discuss cooking with the girls the next week. She was due to have surgery for blood clots in her leg and needed to be quiet in case one broke loose and lodged in her lungs.

Up at Rinconada, I had asked some women to meet me at 3:00 for a charla the next day, and Irma, the little janitor at the puesto, had agreed to go with me. When we arrived at the school, no one was there and I thought, "I have failed." Finally, one woman came, then ten, and by 3:00, twenty women and forty children. I explained about the three food groups and that to be healthy we needed to eat foods from each group. Handing out lottery cards, we spent the next hour playing the nutrition game. Some of the older children took part as well. I wasn't sure whether people came to meet the gringa because they had nothing better to do, or to be polite, but I hoped this would be the beginning of a women's group. We needed a house where we could cook.

EVEN THOUGH BARBARA'S TOWN of Matequescuintla was only fifty miles from Jalapa, it took all day to get out there. My day began at 5:00 in order to board the bus on the corner, and I could hear it honking from up near Rinconada where the driver lived. Chema as usual was glad to see me, and I arrived in Jalapa an hour and a half later. After breakfast at the hotel where Barbara and I had stayed, I picked up a few groceries while waiting for the bank to open. My check finally cleared, and

I had money again.

Barbara's bus appeared dirtier and more dilapidated than mine. I found a seat in the back and buried my nose in a copy of *Jaws*. We drove through a part of Jalapa I had not seen before, some nice houses behind walls. Soon we began to climb and were in the mountains. Unlike the setting where I had come from, everything was green. The bracken fern, cedar and juniper were a nice contrast to the cactus and eucalyptus at my site. As we climbed, the trees became larger and taller, and along the road grew wild, white hydrangeas and orange nasturtiums.

The summit was called *muro mundi*, a view of the world. Later, I found this was virgin timber and was scheduled to become a national park. Small houses constructed of wood dotted the road.

After three and a half hours when the road began its curving descent, it was obvious the bus was unable to make the turn. Women and children were ordered off the bus while the men pushed and pulled to reverse the wheels. I was able to make a needed stop in the bushes. After a half hour of hard work on the part of the men, we were on our way and could see the town far below as we drove one curve after another.

Barbara was waiting for me when I arrived. She had fixed potato salad, pickled vegetables, Vienna sausages, fresh pineapple and excellent coffee with no sugar. Even though Guatemala is one of the prime coffee-growing countries, good coffee is rare. Restaurants often serve Nes Café. In homes that can afford coffee, it is nearly always brewed with sugar, but others brown corn to boil, making a substitute beverage.

It was much colder than Llano Grande and we slept with our sweaters on.

Mateque was a fairly large city with a central park, a large Catholic church, and a *centro de salud* as opposed to my puesto, meaning there were more facilities and personnel.

Barbara had rented a new, concrete-block house which was walled on all sides and contained her landlord's house, a large chicken coop and several outbuildings. She had two rooms, one for a kitchen and eating space and the other for her bedroom. There was a covered patio with her own pila and on one end a room with a cold shower and a toilet with no seat.

Unlike my situation, there had been volunteers there for a number of years and there were three in town at that time. 4-H sent volunteers in pairs, generally a man and a woman. Her co-worker was a young man who had been in my Spanish class, gifted in languages, but too immature to work well in the Peace Corps, we later found out.

We spent the next day exploring the town. The population was perhaps 10,000 with many shops and stores, a bakery that had fresh French bread daily, and an open market for produce. The side streets were cobbled with irregular stones. By afternoon the sun had come out and it was warm enough to wash our hair.

We prepared chicken spaghetti and chocolate pudding for dinner. The cold set in as soon as it was dark at 6:00, and we went to bed early so I could get up at 3:30 for the 4:30 Jalapa bus.

I was glad to arrive early, even though the driver and ayudante were still asleep on the bus. It was dark, but people gradually emerged from the shadows carrying babies and small children, live chickens, and vegetables such as broccoli, beets and potatoes. The odor of wood smoke clung to the clothing of the passengers standing in the aisles.

In the dark bus nearly everyone fell asleep. By the time we left, it was still black outside, and there were at least twenty passengers standing in the aisles. This was market day in Jalapa. We slowly drove up the curving mountain road, and at daybreak the evergreens emerged through the rising mist like trees in a Chinese painting.

Five hours later I was able to shed my sweater and down vest. I bought produce at the market and boarded my bus for home.

There, I swept up several cups of volcanic sand that had accumulated in my absence and washed my clothes by hand. What there wasn't room for on the clothesline, I hung on the wire fence surrounding the chicken yard.

ONE NEVER KNEW how a Peace Corps day would turn out. I knew Maria was in the hospital with phlebitis, so I assumed the meeting I had scheduled the day after my return from Matequescuintla would be canceled, but Linda reminded me everyone was expecting to make banana Incaparina pancakes.

Maria's mother was at her house and told me I needed to buy bananas and flour. I lettered one chart for the wall with the recipe and another for six times the amount.

Not only had sixty girls and women gathered but Linda and Sarita closed the health center to come help.

Although Maria had a traditional adobe wood-burning stove, we used her gas plate. "*Perfecto*," exclaimed Sarita as she turned a round, golden-brown pancake which they called *panqueques*. We served them cold, sprinkled with sugar. Each girl paid a few centavos, for the ingredients, and had the choice of eating them there or taking them home. I was pleasantly surprised to be reimbursed for what I had spent, not so much because I needed the money but it told me I was not being viewed as a wealthy gringa.

Shortly after, I learned how CARE distributed its food. The United States government sends vegetable oil, bulgar wheat and enriched cornmeal to Third World countries. I had heard stories of the food either being sold or fed to animals, but everything was done properly in Llano Grande. Linda arranged for a truck to bring the heavy bags of cereal from Jalapa, and she and Irma spent hours measuring two pounds each in plastic bags. She then contacted the radio station to announce to the village women when the food could be picked up at the puesto.

By 8:00 in the morning there was a long line of women carrying bags, baskets and bottles. Irma poured oil through a funnel and Linda handed out bags of grain. I had prepared a talk on how to store and cook bulgar but decided I would be more helpful handing out food. There were at least 100 women, nearly all of whom had brought babies and young children. A few had children big enough to help carry. Large families received double amounts.

I took a picture of Paulina, a small Indian woman, and her four children. The baby was very malnourished and clutched a filthy bottle. Her red eyes and streaming nose told us she had both conjunctivitis and catarrh. Linda said the alcoholic father had died last year.

One day Linda and I walked to an aldea called Carmen, located a half mile uphill from Llano Grande. Like Rinconada, there was no electricity, and adobe houses surrounded by *milpas* (cornfields) dotted the hillside. Because it was higher than Llano Grande, pines grew as well as lovely huge tropical trees. There were outcroppings of rocks, but everything was much greener than down below.

The schoolhouse sat on a hill covered with slabs of limestone. Inside there was one room furnished with the teacher's desk and benches for the children. Outdoors was a latrine and an enclosure with an adobe stove.

While Linda sprayed the children's heads for lice, Ralfia, the teacher, and I chatted about my coming up to teach some health and nutrition classes.

Afterwards, we stopped at a large house to meet Petronia, one of the area's midwives. Linda told her I would like to start a women's group and asked if I could use her house, and she seemed agreeable.

After two months into our lives as full-fledged volunteers, the nutritionists were summoned to the training center by Sergio. We spent an extremely boring morning listening to a lecture on teaching methods in Spanish from an educator and all agreed it was a total waste of time.

That afternoon I took a bus to Guate to go to the Peace Corps office where I collected fifteen letters, a stack of notices and three *Newsweek* magazines. All volunteers received the Latin American version gratis. I ordered mail to be sent to Llano Grande. In addition, I signed up for a gas stove and a bicycle.

My friends who worked for U.S.A.I.D. in El Salvador had left a CARE package for me of books and food. There was a gigantic can of tuna as well as cereal and candy. As it was too heavy to carry, I left it in Sergio's office with my name on it. It was time as well for a gamma globulin shot, a prevention for hepatitis, and a requirement every four months. I made an appointment to see a dentist, as I had a tooth that was bothering me.

Later, I met Barbara and we left for the airport to meet her daughter Beth, who had come to spend ten days with her mother.

April 1989

Antigua, the old capital, and a wonderful colonial city, celebrates Easter like nowhere else. We were up early to see the *alfrombas*, literally carpets of flowers and elaborate designs made of colored sawdust. All night crews laid out the patterns which were later obliterated by the floats and parades. We were warned to watch for pickpockets as the streets were crowded with tourists as well as Guatemalans watching the proceedings. Brass bands led floats pulled by men carrying Christ on the cross. Mary was carried by girls and women, and the crowd was solemn and reverent.

In the middle of the afternoon there was an announcement that Jesus was about to be put to death and the crucifixion would take three hours. This was getting to be too realistic and too Catholic for me, and I opted out.

Back home in Llano Grande, I attended what I assumed would be Easter services, but they were having a "session" or meeting and I went with Alicia to her Sunday School classes. The children were charming and I was able to understand the Spanish.

Afterwards, in the dining room at home, a handsome young man introduced himself as Alvaro and told me he worked for the Agriculture Department. He had heard I was interested in doing school gardens and offered his help. He made my day!

SHORTLY AFTER THAT I had another visit from Buck who had discovered a six-year-old Indian girl at the Monjas puesto who weighed only seventeen pounds. He had convinced the parents that the child must be hospitalized at the center for malnourished children and they agreed.

Buck had arranged to meet them at 3:00 A.M. several days before and they had not appeared. The reason for the early hour stemmed from the difficulty of getting her to the hospital during admitting hours. He was furious with the nurses and staff at the health center for not having them at the bus stop and told them in no uncertain terms what he thought of them. The bottom line was that I needed to take over as he was leaving for the States for a two-week vacation. I spoke with Linda who suggested I see the social worker at the Jalapa hospital who should be able to arrange transportation.

On an early morning trip to Jalapa, I headed for the hospital, where Linda had taken her nurse's training, in order to ask the social worker's help in getting Gloria, the little Indian girl, to the hospital. I got absolutely nowhere in the hospital. Eventually, Linda was able to make arrangements with people who would help.

The day came for me to take Gloria to the hospital, God willing. Linda's friend, Betty, worked as a nurse at the Monjas health center and had agreed to have me spend the night with her.

When I arrived in Monjas, Rigberto, a large, obese, health worker, whom I had previously met, insisted I ride behind him on his motorcycle to Gloria's home to remind them of our plans. No one was home at their adobe hut with thatched roof, and we returned to the puesto, bouncing over dirt roads and through dry fields. Apparently, the family had misunderstood, as they arrived shortly after us.

Gloria was a pathetic little thing, not much taller than her thirteen-month-old sister. Wearing a yellow organdy dress, pink socks, and new white shoes, she looked at me and scowled. It took her mother, the doctor, the nurse, and me to weigh and measure the child. At seventeen pounds and seventy-three centimeters, she was the most malnourished child I had seen. She neither walked nor talked and her legs and arms resembled little sticks. After she stopped crying, she looked at me and scowled again.

We explained it was necessary to meet the bus by 2:30 A.M., and I gave the father my alarm clock set for 2:00, along with my flashlight. After Buck's experience, I was not at all confident they would come.

Betty, Linda's friend, lived in the back of a pharmacy with an extended family. Her parents were visiting in the States, but I met her sister, a niece, and Betty's precocious four-year-old daughter Beverly.

66

I waited in the living room while the women prepared dinner. An enormous cockroach, bigger than my thumb, scuttled across the tiled floor. I was so used to stepping on them that I did so without thinking and then wondered how to get rid of it, but the problem was solved when an army of ants appeared and carried it off.

Dinner consisted of very tough fried beef, black beans with sour cream, tortillas, sweetened coffee and cookies. I was grateful for their hospitality and told them so.

At 8:00, Betty suggested we go to bed. I had planned to sleep in my slip, but Betty insisted I wear her red satin and lace nightgown. Beverly slept with her mother.

I worried about getting up in time and glanced at the clock each hour. To my horror, at 2:15 the alarm had not rung and I hastily dressed. Betty was a dear and accompanied me to the bus line several blocks away.

The sky was black with a sprinkling of stars and a sliver of a moon. There was no sign of Santos, Gloria's father, or the child, and we waited in silence. I knew they were not coming. Suddenly, there was a speck of light and two figures; one of them, carrying a child, walked toward me. Santos had brought his father. Gloria, wrapped in a blanket, wore the same little yellow dress and a pink sweater.

The bus did not arrive until 3:30, and the three of us sat together while Gloria fell asleep in her father's arms. When it began to get light, the bus was full. Passing through lovely coffee country, I could see clusters of lavender orchids growing high in tall shade trees.

I shared a package of cookies and some oranges with Santos and his father. Gloria had no intention of eating and kept giving me malevolent looks. Four hours later we arrived at the busy terminal where the thief had tried to steal my wallet the previous winter. I hoped my two five-foot men would protect me if necessary. I had trouble finding the San Juan Sacatepéquez bus and argued with an obnoxious cab driver who insisted on driving us there. He was so persistent, I finally shouted, "Shut up!" A nicely dressed college student came to my aid and showed us where to catch our next bus.

Gloria sat on her father's lap scowling (another "face of vinegar" person). I was sure she knew I was responsible for something she would not enjoy. Santos had been given twenty quetzals for bus fare for his father and himself. We drove by lush orchards, fields of chrysanthemums, blue and purple statice, and greenhouses filled with roses to be shipped to florists out of the country.

Arriving at San Juan Sacatepéquez, a woman told me there was no taxi to the hospital but that it was only a short walk. I bought six bananas which we ate while walking the kilometer uphill to the hospital, which is supported by the Lion's Club. The buildings were set in a park surrounded by flowers and trees.

My heart sank when the woman in admittance told us they had had no call from the hospital in Jalapa, but we were told to wait on the porch. A vanload of toddlers were being readied for an outing. Some objected vigorously as they were placed in the vehicle. Boxes of cookies, bananas, rolls, and bottles of milk were packed for the picnic.

Gloria was finally seen by a beautiful woman pediatrician. Refusing to stand to be measured, she began to scream. One thing was certain, there was nothing wrong with her lungs. The doctora examined her carefully. She told me that Gloria was severely retarded, her head was too small, and her brain had not grown. Her reflexes were normal, but her ears were deformed and her teeth were in bad shape, in addition to the extreme

Picture is the corn harvest from which I've taken colors for my quilt.
Rug hides a large crack in the wall.

malnutrition. She would stay at the hospital from four to six months and then either be sent back to her family or to a home for retarded children. They would consult a specialist.

Grandpa had stayed outside, and I wondered how much Santos understood. A nurse arrived with a big towel, removed Gloria's clothes and took her away for a bath. I went with Santos while pages of forms were filled out for him.

Before we left, I asked if we could say good-bye to the child. We were taken to her crib in isolation where Gloria, her hair freshly washed and combed in two pony tails, wore a long-sleeved, white, Victorian dress and was holding a bottle of Incaparina. When she saw her father she cried pitifully. I cried too, although Santos looked stoic and waved as we went out the door. All the way home I told him he had done the right thing and his daughter now had a chance to be a healthy little girl. I never saw Gloria again, but I was told she had returned home plump and in good health.

One Saturday I shopped at the market for furnishings for my nine-by-twelve room. I bought two straw mats to cover the concrete floor and more baskets for sewing, mail, laundry, and magazines. In the flower section I found purple statice and a pottery vase.

My room really looked quite inviting. The floor to ceiling bookcase had come, for which I had paid twenty-five dollars, and I was able to stack books, boxes of teaching materials, food, dishes and kitchen utensils on the shelves. I spread a maroon tablecloth on my bed and covered the table with a piece of Mayan weaving in shades of pink, purple, turquoise and blue. The crack on the wall behind my bed was hidden behind the cotton rug.

Everyone admired the decorating and Grandmother stopped to gaze every time she passed my door.

All week I weighed and measured babies and small children. I had made a growth chart for the wall, which made it easy to clarify which category into which they fell. We had regular scales and baby scales, both of which measured in pounds, but height was measured in centimeters. Babies were laid in a wooden box with a board pushed against their feet for determining length. Most objected noisily.

That day there were nine children in the yellow category, signaling danger, and five in the red, meaning very serious. A young mother brought in a young four-pound baby whom she said she was still breast feeding. She

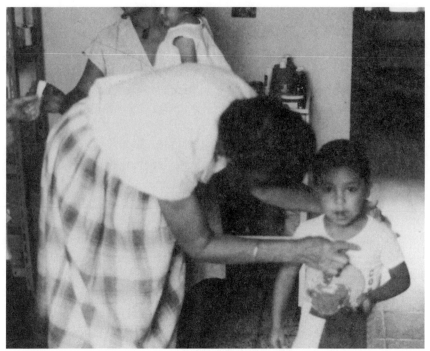

Sticker for being weighed and measured

was obviously failing to thrive. We told the mother the baby needed to be hospitalized, but she refused. Sarita told her to give the child Incaparina mixed with water. Shortly afterward, we heard that the baby had died.

ONE SATURDAY MORNING when I arrived in Jalapa I was able to reach two of my sons by telephone. What a lift to be able to connect with home!

On the street I met two volunteers I had heard about but hadn't met. June and Barry from Washington, D.C., were about thirty and had been working for six months in a program called Appropriate Technology in which they built ovens, stoves, latrines or water systems. I told them I was meeting Barbara when her bus came in, and they invited us to their house for lunch.

The couple lived on the edge of town about a mile from the shopping center. They showed us the solar dryer they had made, an outdoor oven and a "chef stove" designed to use a minimum of wood. They had planted a garden and proudly pointed out that they were a "two-pila" family—one inside and the other on the back porch.

We had brought a melon and pastry and June fixed a sweet and sour vegetable soup with Protemas (another soy meat substitute) and garlic bread. During lunch Barry told us about the tapeworm with which he had just parted company. Volunteers, I learned, were not at all reticent in discussing the condition of their bowels or any worms or other parasites they harbored.

Back shopping, I bought cotton fabric in pastel colors for a quilt I planned to make for my bed. There were two cinemas in town but nothing was showing we cared to see.

Sunday morning I stocked up on cookies, pickles, packaged pudding, chocolate and tuna at the supermercado which was a dreadfully dirty store. June had told us about a cleaner store near the bus depot where she bought powdered milk, cheese, lunch meat and ice cream cones. At the big market I purchased *jocotes*, a plum-like fruit, cantaloupe, a small watermelon, limes, carrots, beets and radishes. Reluctantly, I boarded my morning bus. For two days I had spoken mostly English.

The next day I was able to sleep until 7:00, having become immune to being awakened by roosters and barking dogs. However, the absence of the usual bus honking was due to the fact it had broken down.

At the health center I drew a large chart for the wall from my notes on food for babies the first year. I stressed that if possible an infant should be breast fed for two years, but for that to happen the mother must be well nourished.

To the tune of *Pop Goes the Weasel*, I wrote my first song to be sung in school. It translated to:

Milk and eggs, meat and beans, Incaparina build and repair the body. Carumba, growth group! Oranges, Swiss chard, turnips, lemons, melons, tomatoes have vitamins and minerals. Carumba, protection group! Oil, bananas, noodles, cereal, avocados, sugar and bread make the body work well. Carumba, Energy!

My own children would have been embarrassed, as I neither sing well nor play the guitar. I planned to ask Alicia and Israel, who played the

71

guitar at church, to sing it so I could record it on my tape recorder.

At the puesto I prepared bulgar wheat salad and confiscated all of Linda's spoons and forks so the women could sample the salad. I was surprised when Linda plopped a spoonful of bulgar on her palm and ate it that way. All the women followed her example.

Linda showed me her paycheck, which was under the equivalent of 200 American dollars and then deductions for medical care. She asked me what I made and I told her about the same, although I lied a little. We made some over that, had vacation money set aside for us, complete medical and dental care, and a bonus when we left after two years.

That night there was a worship service in the dining room next to my room. I felt sorry for the minister's four young children who had to stay up late with their parents at least five nights out of seven.

THE NEXT DAY BARBARA ARRIVED at Llano Grande on the noon bus. I had cleaned my room in anticipation. While we ate our lunch of ham, cheese, and avocado sandwiches, iced tea and cantaloupe, Grandma, who sat at the head of the table, said nothing, but did not take her eyes off of us. Barbara asked if she would watch us in silence the whole

Emaciated cow

meal, and I answered, "Yes."

We toured the aldea, the dusty unpaved roads covered with animal droppings. Garbage, such as plastic bags and straw, was strewn along the edge of the street, and emaciated cows, pigs and goats wandered looking for something to eat.

Because my town was so much smaller than Mateque, a visitor was more obvious, and everyone was curious to see another gringa. Barbara had met friendly Linda on the bus. She invited us to see her crocheting, knitting and embroidery work. I wished I had a house of my own with more space, but both Alicia and Chusita made my guest feel welcome.

Sunday morning we caught the usual 6:00 A.M. bus for Jalapa where we had panqueques, orange juice and coffee and then headed for the market. I was home by noon, but it took Barbara six hours to get to her village.

The next day Linda was gone for the morning, and I wrote a thank-you note to Betty in Monjas where I had stayed the night before taking Gloria to the hospital. I took four weeks of lesson plans to Aida and told her I was ready to begin teaching the following week. The afternoon was a 4-H Club day. I had planned to make unbaked chocolate oatmeal cookies with the girls, but there was no oatmeal. Instead, the girls wanted to play Nutrition Bingo, and a group walked home with me to play some more on Chusita's patio. I had begun piecing on my quilt and the girls watched with interest. It would have been fun to do some quilting with them, but I was afraid the fabric would be too expensive.

There had been thunder all day, and in the afternoon we had a two-hour downpour. The oil drums used for catching rainwater were overflowing, which meant there would be plenty of water for a while. It had cooled down and everything smelled fresh.

ISRAEL, FROM THE CHURCH, came over with his guitar for a "taping session." He and Alicia sang a duet in harmony of the *Three Food Groups* song, and their singing was good. During the recording a loud buzzing began. I had only read of cicadas in books. Whether the rain brought them to life, or it was the season, their buzzing was so loud we had to go inside my room and shut the door. Not knowing what they were, I had wondered if there was a problem with the town's electricity. In addition, the singing aroused Grandmother's caged parakeet and he squawked loudly, adding to the din.

Behind closed doors, we held our taping session, recording all three verses. The next week I would try it out in school.

SEVERAL DAYS LATER, I awakened with the terrible feeling I had an abscessed tooth and not the one for which I had the appointment. Arriving at the Peace Corps office around noon, I picked up my dental x-rays and checked into the Spring Hotel where volunteers are piled into rooms regardless of age or gender.

Within walking distance was a store where I had been told I could buy a four-inch foam pad to use as a mattress. Negotiating the purchase was no problem, but carrying it was a different matter. It was rolled and tied, but I could hardly get my arm around it to carry it. I looked so ridiculous. I felt as though I was taking part in a *Pink Panther* movie. Back at the hotel I found I was sharing a room with Ellen from my nutrition group and Kelly, Barbara's site partner in 4-H up at Matequescuintla. My tooth felt worse and hurt most of the night.

By morning my cheek was red, swollen and throbbing. Ellen and I had breakfast together, and I took a cab to the dentist as I couldn't handle the mattress on a city bus. The cab driver was most solicitous and said he had trouble with his teeth too. He wasn't exaggerating, for when we arrived at the dentist's office he wished me good luck and gave me a wide smile exposing his one tooth!

I parked the great piece of foam in the waiting room and was ushered into Dr. Hans Klienshmit's office. Although he was Guatemalan, he obviously had German roots. A number of Germans in the late 1800s settled in the country and raised coffee. Dr. Klienshmit's English was excellent. He agreed I did have an abscess which would get worse by the hour unless I had a root canal. There was only one dentist who did this procedure and he hoped he would be in town. Bravely, I asked what would happen if he were on vacation, and he patted me on the shoulder "assuring" me he would drill a hole to drain the pus, which he pronounced "*poos.*"

I was in luck as the other dentist could see me late in the afternoon, although his office was on the other side of the city. The Camino Real was close by, and I felt I deserved to pamper myself. There was a long wait to get into my room, but I was given an embassy rate. I would have liked to have taken a nap, as I had had little sleep the previous night, but felt I needed time to get across town.

The new dentist had been trained in Paris and spoke Spanish and French but did not speak English. I spent a miserable two hours as the anesthetic wore off while he x-rayed every few minutes. By his body language I could tell things were not going well. The only pleasant experience was that he listened to classical music while he worked. He finally finished and gave me prescriptions for penicillin and codeine and told me to return on Monday.

At the pharmacy near the hotel I was able to buy penicillin, but not codeine, and asked for a pill for the pain. On the corner stand I bought a Sprite, which the vendor poured into a plastic bag and inserted a straw, as is the custom, and explained why the whole country is littered. Noting my swollen cheek, he commiserated with me.

Sunday I felt much better and attended the English-speaking Protestant church I had been to with my friends from home. There were no Peace Corps volunteers that day, but the service was familiar and comfortable.

As a reward to myself for my problems, I bought a black swim suit and some silver earrings and spent the afternoon at the pool where I managed to get sunburned.

Dreading another session with the root canal specialist, and because of my gigantic foam pad, again I took a cab. The dentista reported my tooth looked fine and told me to return in two weeks. The mattress rode on the top of the bus to Jalapa. Fortunately, it was a sunny day.

I WAS NERVOUS about my first day at school. There were fifty children in Aida's first grade class. I discussed the three food groups and distributed crayons and paper for them to draw fruits and vegetables. Most of them had never held either a pencil or crayon, so I made drawings of some of the foods and let the children color inside the lines.

The third graders were easier. The students were able to draw pictures, and we sang the *Three Food Groups* song along with the tape. We played a game where I tossed a ball to a child, named a food group, and he tried to tell me a food from that group. The class had fun and so did I.

Seven girls came over to my patio to trace drawings with carbon paper for coloring and stayed until dark. I was brushing my teeth the next morning at 6:45 when Ingrid, a rather large pushy girl, arrived at my door to color. I wasn't sure whether she really wanted to work or to report on what I did before 7:00 A.M.

MARIA INVITED ME to her home for lunch to see a demonstration by a home economist and her helper-in-training from the extension office. The women baked meatloaf in the toaster oven and prepared rice, tortillas, and cucumber salad. In addition, they fried bayonet flowers from a tall yucca-type plant that grew there. I had tried them before and found them bitter. The beverage was Kool-Aid and the helper fixed an elaborate pie made of cornflakes, margarine, sugar, and vanilla, over which she poured sweetened condensed milk and beaten eggs. The result was sweet and sticky, but the most adventurous cooking I had eaten in the village.

CHUSITA'S BROTHER, Cristobal, was a sometime roomer at the house. I thought he might have had my room before I came. He was an unattractive little man with thick black brows and apparently was unemployed. At first he tried to talk to me using a few "cutesy" English words he knew. He told me he had five children around Guatemala City and his wife was in the States studying "Bible." As I got to know him better I could understand why she stayed there.

Chusita was enthusiastic about my planting a garden and said Cristobal would do the digging. I had seeds from the Peace Corps office and bought a rake. Each time I told him I was ready to begin, I got an evasive answer and finally got hostile looks. I had begun to dislike him intensely and wrote to my friend Pat at home that he reminded me of a large black beetle and I felt like stepping on him with my Birkenstocks, only maybe he really would dig the garden and then I would be sorry!

Admitting to me that her brother really did not like to work, Chusita hired a man to do the spading. He had a difficult time as the whole garden area was teeming with fire ants. As a Northerner, I had never had experience with them. They were numerous, tiny, and left painful stings that itched and burned for several days. I had brought garden gloves from home and secured the cuffs of my long-sleeved shirt and the bottoms of my jeans with rubber bands to keep them from crawling up my arms and legs.

ONE MORNING I walked up and down a hill, crossed the river by walking over flat rocks, and proceeded a kilometer past a tobacco curing shed to the school in Rinconada. I was particularly fond of Rosemary, the teacher, a pretty Guatamalteca with dark eyes and wavy hair who generally wore jeans. Rosemary always reinforced what I said to her students, which I appreciated.

When I returned, I was so tired and hot that I consumed two orange sodas. Chusita was frantically looking for the mail bag she had brought from the Monjas post office. She had set it inside the counter in the farmacia and gone to her room for a few minutes. When she returned, the bag was missing. Nearly every family had someone working in the U.S. and they often sent money home. Any mail I might have received was missing as well and none of it ever surfaced.

I HAD BEEN EXPERIMENTING with different methods of cooking bulgar wheat, which was one of the CARE products, and came up with a particularly good dish using a Spanish rice recipe with Protemas, a meat substitute, fresh tomatoes, tomato sauce, onion, raisins and cinnamon. It was a winner.

One busy day at the health center I helped hand out CARE products all morning. After lunch when I walked back to work it was very hot, and I spent the afternoon reading in Spanish—material from the ministry of health and a Peace Corps book on gardening in the tropics. Suddenly, the temperature dropped, there was a strong wind, hail, and then sheets of rain. It was an hour before I could run home. Linda had a Talbot's catalog and we looked at clothes we would like to buy.

It was so cold when I arrived home that I put on a wool sweater and made a pot of tea. I even gave Cristobal a cup. Alicia, Eloisa and I sat in my room drinking tea and listening to Grieg's *Peer Gynt* suite on tape. They didn't say they enjoyed the music, but it was a nice change from constant hymns, at least for me.

The next day I had an appointment to finish the root canal, and the dentista kept me waiting an hour before completing the procedure without Novocain and it was over. Later at the Peace Corps office the nurse who had given me the bad time just before I left for Llano Grande upbraided me for going to a pharmacy for penicillin the dentist had prescribed, rather than the office. I reminded her the office was closed, I had a raging infection, and could not wait until the weekend was over, but she remained unimpressed. Later, we were all glad to learn she had been fired.

On MY WAY HOME via Jalapa, I sat at the Chinese Chicken restaurant with two volunteers, one of whom was from Barbara's village. Because Johanna's bus did not leave until after noon the following day, I invited her home with me. While we were eating, there was a heavy rainstorm. Water came over the curbs, and we had to take off our shoes in order to cross the street.

Johanna was a young pretty blond with a peaches-and-cream complexion and was a little on the plump side. Her program was animal husbandry, and she said she was constantly hassled by both farmers and employees from the Agricultural Department. Chema took one look and immediately fell in love. He solicitously helped her on the bus, assisted her getting off, and for months asked me when she would be coming back. Even though it was nearly dark when we arrived, all of Llano Grande knew I had a beautiful blond guest. The next morning I put her on the 6:00 A.M. bus, and Chema and the driver took her to Jalapa.

THERE WAS A THREE-MONTH REPORT due for Sergio to be completed in Spanish. I was required to track down all sorts of trivia, such as whether husbands ate first and women and children had what was left, or how many families out of ten used birth control. As I hadn't a clue, I needed Linda to help me out. She said some men ate first and about two families out of ten used contraception.

That afternoon she and I walked to a town I hadn't visited called Piedro del Fuego, or rocks of fire, because of the abundance of flintstone. We walked two-and-a- half miles, crossed a river, passed several affluent farm houses, and followed a dusty unpaved road through fields, forest, and the

78

bend of the river to a schoolhouse. Linda sprayed forty black heads for lice while I chatted with Freddy, the teacher, a delightful young man. Someone had brought a radio, and the older students had a wonderful time dancing.

On our way home we stopped at a farm house for scrambled eggs, sweetened coffee and tortillas prepared by a friend of Linda's. She seemed to know everyone and was well liked. Often they gave her plants and cuttings. Even the poorest homes had house plants in pots or cans on the edges of their patio or flowers in cans nailed outside the house.

One day at 4-H Club Maria and Linda invited me to a party that they told me would be all women and with lots of *bromas* (jokes) and laughing. Dark clouds had formed, and I quickly took my clothes off the line and showered before my solar shower cooled off. Great drops of rain began to fall and cracks of thunder echoed in the hills. In an hour the streets were a mire of slippery mud, and I decided not to go to the fiesta in the dark unless someone came for me.

Shortly afterward, Linda and Maria arrived in a truck, and we drove several blocks to a house with a tienda in front and a nice patio and living quarters in the rear. As we parked on the street in the dark and made our way through the oozy mud, someone lit a string of firecrackers and an attractive señorita wearing a yellow, satin, off-the-shoulder dress opened the door. She appeared both surprised and embarrassed. As the party progressed, it dawned on me that this was a bridal shower.

The bride-to-be was named Wilma, pronounced *Vilma*. So that she would know what to expect on her wedding night, with gales of laughter, she was handed a plate containing a French roll on which rested an enormous frankfurter and two hard-boiled eggs sprinkled with feathers. I learned later the vernacular for testicles was *huevos* (eggs). There was much giggling as Wilma nibbled on an egg.

Next we dressed the bride in sheaths of toilet paper, complete with bouquet. The women insisted I be the first to dance with her, and all twenty-five girls and women had a turn. We were expected to ask questions about the upcoming wedding night, but with my shaky Spanish, I wisely remained silent.

Refreshments were fried tortillas spread with black beans and mayonnaise. There was clapping after each gift—such as a plastic cup or strainer—was presented. I would have gladly brought something had I known what was going on. An experience to be remembered!

GRANDMA FELL AGAIN for the second time. It was a good thing I was home as she was unable to get up by herself. The poor thing needed a walker.

I went to school prepared to do a charla on a balanced diet and found there were no lessons, as they were involved in making Mother's Day posters. The counter at Linda and Alfonso's tienda was full of dishes and artificial flowers to be sold for gifts.

Sarita took me to Terrones, the aldea a mile below Llano Grande, which appeared more affluent and was situated on a hill surrounded by trees. There was a school there as well, where I thought perhaps I could teach.

We attended the 4-H meeting in a nice house perched up high with a view of the valley below. Sarita talked to the girls about nutrition and health, and I about a balanced diet. The girls were well-dressed and attentive and we then played lotteria. The next day on my way to the puesto I met Maria carrying an enormous chocolate sheet cake for the school. Because all the schools I had planned to visit were involved with Mother's Day, I spent my time making a large wall graph where we could quickly compare children's weight and age.

Sarita invited me to her home in Monjas for dinner. In the front was a store selling fertilizer, pesticides and veterinary supplies. Their living quarters were the most modern I had seen in Guatemala. The floors were covered with rugs, the furniture was upholstered, and the windows had draperies. In the living room was a grand piano and the kitchen had a sink instead of a pila, cabinets, and modern appliances. A classmate of Sarita's doing his residency in Monjas joined us for dinner. Her mother served us beef stuffed with vegetables, two salads, a roasted chicken we were too full to eat, toast and hot chocolate. On the way home thousands of fire flies flashed their lights before another torrential rain began.

With the heavy rains, Chusita's garden began to bloom. There was lavender crepe myrtle, red and yellow canna lilies, along with a pink shrimp plant, hibiscus and red bougainvillea. The potted ferns hanging under the patio roof were six feet long.

BARBARA AND I MET on the highway fifty miles from the capital to explore a town on the Pacific coast called Monterrico. We rode a total of five buses and took a small boat for a ten-minute trip through a waterway. These were the lowlands, an extremely hot and humid area which was a nature preserve for the huge sea turtles who come to lay their eggs in November and December.

The hotel was run by a former volunteer who explained she had owned it for six months and had ideas for improvement. The wide porch that faced the ocean was lined with hammocks. Nancy, the owner, said often the water was like a mill pond, but that day there was a high surf, and as much as I would have liked to have gone swimming I was wary.

We dined on fried shark and slept under netting which made things even hotter. That night there were no cool ocean breezes.

In the morning we walked back to town to bargain for a boat to go out on the waterway dotted with small islands and grassy hummocks. Wading roseate spoonbills, as pink as strawberry ice cream, were feeding along with cormorants who stood drying their wings. An eagle with a fish in his beak and a hawk I was unable to identify soared at the sound of the motor.

Back at the hotel we met John, a fisheries volunteer, whose project was raising shrimp. He was petting Nancy's puppy, a huge coal-black dog with feet the size of teacups. His breed was mastiff and Zimbabwean razorback, and John suggested he looked like a dog who perhaps had come up from hell.

Later, John, who was at least six-foot-three and weighed over two hundred pounds, came up from the beach white and shaking. He said he had been caught in three rollers, and even though he had worked as a lifeguard, he would not have survived a fourth wave.

It was a good thing we had taken our weekly dose of chloroquin, a malaria preventative, as mosquitoes and other biting insects were everywhere.

On the way home we attended our first annual security meeting held in each district, ours near the El Salvadorian border. We met at a hotel designed for us as a "safe house" in case of emergencies. About twenty-five of us ate lunch of fried chicken, salad, soft drinks and ice cream with the Peace Corps director and assistant. We were briefed on Guatemalan politics or any problems they felt might occur, but nothing extraordinary seemed to be in the offing.

THE MIDDLE OF MAY was extremely hot with no water to spare for washing clothes. When I walked up to the aldea of Carmen to give a talk on nutrition, I brought my laundry hoping there would be water at the communal faucet. There was not a drop, and I wondered where their source for essentials such as drinking and cooking came from. Farther down the trail, I waded out in the river and washed some underwear and blouses, but the river was so muddy my things looked worse than before.

When I returned home, Chusita handed me a telegram from a town on the El Salvador border saying there was a *paqueta* for me at customs that I would need to claim in person. Chusita said that Cristobal would accompany me. My first reaction was that I would rather go alone, but decided perhaps he would be of some help and we would be on a friendlier basis.

I thought Cristobal would sit with me on the bus, but he took another seat. After half an hour, we got off at the highway to catch a bus going east to a city called El Progresso, and it was clear he expected me to pay as he plopped down on a front seat and pointed back toward me with a pudgy bitten thumb when the helper came to collect fares. We changed buses again for the frontera and drove through several nice towns. It was extremely pretty country; the road ran along a river shaded with green trees covered with vines.

Just before an arch leading to El Salvador, we came to a large area lined with tables stacked with clothing, fabric, shoes and household goods. Apparently El Salvadorans came there to shop.

Wandering around the tables of clothes, pots and pans, and boom boxes were heavily-made-up, miniskirted girls who eyed each man who walked by. I trailed behind Cristobal who bought himself a bag of sticky candy and a cold soda. As Chusita had told me she wouldn't be handling any mail for the next two months, I mailed some letters at customs. We found the proper rooms for claiming packages, which I could have done on my own, and the officer handed me my paqueta containing knitting patterns and some powdered lemonade I had requested from a friend. The man seemed satisfied that the powder was *lemonada* (lemonade).

Cristobal was totally unwilling to explain anything to me, initiate conversation, or to be agreeable. Again, on the return trip, he sat by himself, pointing a grubby thumb toward me when it was time to pay the fare. I shared a seat with a young nun wearing a white habit who had recently eaten a great deal of garlic. On the window side I was constantly sprinkled with water from baskets of immense pop-eyed fish stowed on the top of the bus.

My sour companion failed to tell me he had shopping to do for Chusita at El Progresso, which took the better part of an hour. At the store he consumed several more soft drinks and bought himself more candy.

At home, I shared the knitting patterns with Maria for 4-H, as there were ideas for knitted bags, hair bands and baby sweaters.

There was so little water for a bath that I used only a small pan of water.

LINDA INVITED ME TO COME with her to her parents' home, adding that there was plenty of water to bathe and wash our hair. While she shopped for meat to take home, I bought school supplies and some red carnations for her mother.

We hired a taxi which took us ten kilometers on the north side of Jalapa along an unpaved dusty road. The house was adobe with cement floors, no electricity, and water from a covered well. Carman, Linda's mother, greeted me with a hug and a kiss and insisted we sit down to a lunch of chicken vegetable soup, fresh tortillas, lemonade, and mangoes.

The farm encompassed eight acres with everything in its proper place. Chickens and doves were in cages, two horses grazed in an adjoining pasture, the vegetable garden was flourishing, as were banana, orange and lemon trees in the orchard.

A neighbor came over to take home my clothes to wash, which was a pleasant surprise, and both Linda and I washed our hair. As I was starting to strip down to my underwear, Carman took me to an enclosed bathhouse where I could wash in privacy.

The taxi returned for us promptly at 2:00, and with clean clothes, washed hair, and full stomachs we returned to Jalapa.

Driving through dusty hills, I saw bright orange flowers on the poinciana trees, and as the bus began the ascent to Llano Grande, a flock of cattle egrets soared into the sunset, their pure white feathers reflecting both pink and blue.

May was mango season. We had been told there were different varieties and they were delicious. My only experience was a juicy, hard-to-eat fruit leaving strings in my teeth. Mangoes sold on the street the last few months resembled little green apples which people dipped in salt. Linda and Alfonso had planted two trees outside the puesto by the pila. I had watched them grow from tiny green beads to large fruits. To my delight, these had no strings and were better than a Washington State peach.

SERGIO, MY NO-NONSENSE Guatemalan-Chinese pediatrician supervisor, sent a telegram stating he was coming for his first visit. I was up by 6:00, showered by pouring cold water over myself, dressed in a clean white blouse and put on silver earrings. I scrubbed the table with Ajax, hoping there was nothing to attract small ants. He arrived at the health center promptly at one minute to 9:00.

I shared my concerns regarding mothers unable to nurse, and he suggested a wet nurse. If that failed, the child could be given Incaparina. He agreed with me that formula could not sit around unrefrigerated, and he seemed pleased with my teaching schedule. We drove to a small village several miles away where Linda and Sarita had set up a vaccination station at the school. Sergio enjoyed meeting Freddy, the teacher, and helping with a piñata Linda had brought as a reward for the children who had received shots.

Back at my house we had chicken-pineapple salad, rolls, lemonade and watermelon. Sergio quietly said grace before lunch and said he was a practicing Catholic. Guatemala is considered a Catholic country, but there are many Protestant churches, mainly Evangelical.

He had a long talk with both Linda and Chusita and reported that she was pleased to have me living there. She was embarrassed over the lack of water, and added I was very careful of its use. Chusita said our water came from Terrones, where it was pumped to our system, but turned off if and when they felt there wasn't enough.

Linda reported to him something very frightening she had not told me. La Provencia was an aldea I had visited only once. Someone started a rumor that I was at the health center to steal babies to take back to the United States. What better position could I be in for finding healthy babies to export! I was both sad and horrified. My Spanish was at the point not good enough to pursue it. Later, I found this tale had been circulated throughout the whole country. Several years later a woman from Alaska was accused of this and critically beaten up in the coffee country.

Sergio suggested I hold training sessions for teachers and let them teach nutrition under my direction. I didn't tell him I didn't think that would happen but I would continue teaching and working with the midwives and health promoters.

I had put my name in for a bicycle which Sergio brought, a beautiful and expensive man's mountain bike. Even though I am five foot eight, the seat was so high I couldn't reach the pedals. I had only ridden a woman's bike but never one with gears. I had trouble throwing my leg over the bar, and since none of the streets were paved, I wondered if a bike was a good idea.

The day after Sergio's departure, Alvaro, the agricultural representative, and I went to school early to talk about school gardens. Everyone thought it was a good idea, but the teachers felt the soil was too poor and the kids were apt to trample the plants. We compromised on using some land close to the puesto. I needed to buy tools, as no one seemed to have any. I could get all the seed I wanted from the Peace Corps office.

The rest of the day I spent climbing the hill and walking to the schools, first at Carmen and then at Rinconada. I had outlines of vegetables and fruits for the children to color. Beautiful and friendly Rosemary had forty children in her room, and I found to my chagrin I was short twelve papers. As the round trip was at least four miles up and down hills and across a river, I always returned hot, dusty and thirsty. As usual, I rewarded myself with two bottles of cold soda pop, called *aguas* there.

One day when Linda was out of the health center vaccinating children, I spent a morning in my own garden. In addition to Swiss chard, beans, beets, spinach, carrots and sweet corn, I planted seeds that one can't grow in my part of Washington, such as cantaloupe and eggplant. I hoped there would be enough rain as there was no way to water except by hand.

THERE WAS EXCITEMENT in Jalapa on Saturday when I met Barbara. President Cherazo's wife, Rochelle, was running for president. There was a van with loudspeakers which attracted crowds of people to where she stood on the steps of the hospital. She appeared very Spanish, fair skinned and beautifully groomed and dressed. She spotted us in the crowd and waved. We called out, "*Buenos suertes*" (good luck).

Barbara and I had noticed a Swiss restaurant on the highway just south of Jalapa that looked interesting. A nice surprise, the dining room had clean red-tiled floors, white ruffled curtains and a charming owner. It was a mistake, however, to have ordered grilled beef, as it was tough as leather. A little half-grown cat sat expectantly under my chair hoping to be fed. I had become accustomed to seeing Guatemalans with no front teeth, but not cats. I wondered how she could manage the tough piece I fed her unless she gummed it or else she had very good molars!

As our regular hotel was full, we spent the night at a pensión where the walls were like paper. Barbara's bus was parked outside, and she was able to secure a seat at 4:30 A.M. and not have to wait and wander around in the dark until the bus left at 5:00.

I slept in until 7:00 and walked over to June and Barry's for breakfast. They too had heard the rumor about gringos stealing babies, but added it was for body parts. One of the Guatemalan women working extension was spreading the story.

I HAD BOUGHT EACH OF THE SIXTH GRADERS a notebook to take notes and make drawings. I asked them to draw a healthy stalk of corn and a sick one, and then a healthy boy or girl and an unhealthy one. Some of them really got into the spirit of making the sick boy look alarmingly thin with greenish tinged skin. They liked singing the *Three Food Groups* song and playing a game with the ball that I had done with Aida's first graders. Alvaro came by to recruit boys for digging up our school garden. Apparently, girls were exempt or else didn't want to take part.

One day Linda said we were to walk to Terrones, a mile away. We visited a mother with four malnourished young children. Linda gave the mother some iron pills, and I suggested giving the children four or five small meals a day and adding a little oil to their beans and cereal. I added if there were a friend or relative close by who had a baby perhaps she would be willing to breast feed the toddler.

We called on Elenora, a midwife about my age, who I strongly suspected might be a *bruja* (witch doctor). The family were good friends of Linda's and insisted on our having coffee and tortillas. While we sat chatting on the patio, a woman brought a young girl whom she said suffered from indigestion and no appetite. Elenora produced a rum bottle filled with vile looking green liquid which she poured into a large glass and had the girl drink. She then pushed her hand against the child's stomach, rubbing in circles to mix it well. "Hands-on medicine," I thought. On the way home, laughing, Linda pushed my stomach around pretending to mix a homemade concoction. She said the girl most likely had worms.

We stopped by a house where Linda's seamstress, Marta, lived. Marta had lived in Texas for several years and had brought back a lovely new model Elgin sewing machine. I decided to buy some material and have her make me a cool cotton dress.

That evening Linda gave me two tamalitos, literally small tamales made of cornmeal mush, wrapped in corn husks, filled with *chipilin* and steamed. I was anxious to try *chipilin*, a legume that grows wild in the mountains. In training, Mario had told us his brother-in-law had done research on the plant for a Ph.D. paper and found that besides being very high in vitamins it contained protein. I had seen it in the market and knew it grew where the weather was *chipi chipi* (misty), hence the name *chipilin*. After sampling it, to my taste it was not a gourmet dish, but certainly a healthy one.

One day at the puesto Linda showed me a small two-month-old baby and then handed me another just like him. The twins were named Hilmer and Hervet, and the mother, who had lost several babies in the past, was over forty. She appeared extremely clean and mixed a formula from powdered milk with boiled water from a thermos. I fed Hilmer his bottle but was unable to get him to burp. I was told the Spanish word was *hipo* or sometimes *aire* (air). We suggested she add a little oil and sugar to the formula.

Santos came in with four of her children. She lived in Llano Grande with an alcoholic husband. All of the children were in the "red zone" of being severely malnourished when we marked them on the growth chart.

WITHIN A YEAR AFTER TRAINING, we were entitled to a week of Spanish classes and I headed for Santa Lucia. I couldn't face staying with Estella and her children, so I stopped at the home where Barbara had lived to ask if I would be able to board there for a week. The girls said there was a trainee named Roberto but they had an extra bed and their mother would be delighted to have me stay.

Back to studying Spanish was fun. My teacher had a Peace Corps girl friend, his English was good, and he said he was able to think in English, although he always conversed in Spanish. Outside the classroom hung pots of geraniums where courting blue and purple hummingbirds hovered.

Mario, my trainer, was glad to see me. I told him about the twins and he said they should be on a Similac-type formula. I stopped by Estella's house only to find her in bed hooked up to an I.V. She cried when she saw me, and her doctor came by while I was there. I thought Irving was exceptionally naughty and didn't find the other boys particularly friendly.

The following morning I was covered with insect bites, as Barbara had been when she lived there. The bugs must have been getting stronger all the time with the constant stream of volunteers on which they fed!

After class I took a bus to Antigua where I bought brownies for Estella and the children and had dinner with Marion. Because neither of us wanted to go home in the dark, I left early.

The poor husband of my hostess was in bad shape. He was in bed the week I was there. Barbara had mentioned he had diabetes, and he now had an infected foot. He showed me his medicine telling me it contained dried snake.

OVER THE WEEKEND, Peace Corps sponsored a bird count at Puerto Barrios near huge Lake Izabal on the Caribbean. A young woman also taking Spanish was going and asked me to go with her. Karen wanted to stay at the Tranquilidad in Guate, which was an old firetrap hotel occupied by prostitutes on the first floor. Our rooms were on the third floor "penthouse" where there was water only in the morning. At noon a torrential downpour lasted several hours.

I was able to do some shopping, having heard about a hardware store where one could buy blocks of imported German chocolate. Across the street was a spice store where I purchased cinnamon, cloves, and pepper, and on the corner a seed store that had parsley, lettuce, spinach and basil for my garden.

Karen and I left the capital the next morning by 6:30 for the six-hour trip to the lake. We had lunch at Hotel Barrios and walked to a natural pool in the rocks fed by some cool springs. It was humid and the temperature was in the 100°s. We sat on the Atlantic beach until another rainstorm forced us to a covered shelter. The rest of the group arrived, and we ordered rice, shrimp, fried platanos and tomato salad from a restaurant in the park.

The group consisted of mostly forestry volunteers, all of whom were under twenty-five. I seemed to be accepted. Someone named Tom had arranged for us to stay at his house for the night, and I slept comfortably on Tom's sleeping bag on the floor.

We were out by 4:00, a good time to see birds, as they begin to feed as soon as it is light. I was paired with two young men, Jim and Dan, who really were not "hard core" birders and good about hauling me over logs and steep places when necessary. I had birded in many places in the world and found I knew more what the birds "were not" than what "they were." I had *Peterson's Guide to Mexican Birds*, and we identified grackles and cowbirds but saw a hummer I couldn't find in the book. We looked for toucans, asking some boys if they had seen any, but they said they were generally around but not that day.

By 1:00 it was so hot we returned home to take a nap and cool off. The second night we all stayed in the summer home of a doctor who had befriended one of the men. The house was built by a small waterfall that made pools in the rocks below, large enough for us to swim in. The house was surrounded by trees and flowering plants.

I finally met David, the volunteer who had lived at Estella's house before I came. There was also a girl from Colorado who had worked with my son Jeff in Outward Bound there.

David and three of the women and I hiked a long way to town in the midday heat where we caught a cab and then a bus for the city.

I ATTENDED 4-H ON Monday. Sarita, with the aid of an overhead projector, talked to the girls about hygiene and first aid. From Maria, I learned the teachers had been on strike for a week and most likely would be the next week as well. In addition, the post office was still on strike.

The only good news was that my Swiss chard was up. The compound was walled on one side with the farmacia and rooms on the other two so that neighboring animals weren't browsing in the garden. A herd of goats, led by a particularly smelly Billie, wandered about eating from anyone's yard that they fancied.

One morning as I waited for the bus to take me to Guate, I heard an unearthly sound behind a neighbor's fence. I peaked through the slats and

The wandering billie goat

saw a woman with a large butcher knife in her hand standing over a large trussed pig stretched out on a board. Just as she began the process of castrating him, the bus arrived, sparing me from having to watch the procedure.

In LLANO GRANDE, the CARE program required the recipients to be weighed and measured every three months. In spite of the heat, all of the babies wore crocheted booties and most wore woolen caps, so their hair was plastered to their little heads with perspiration. In addition, they were swathed in blankets. Normally, I had time to play with them, but that morning there were at least fifty babies, most of whom screamed the minute I picked them up. Sarita agreed we sounded as though we were torturing them.

One one-year-old girl weighed only eight pounds. She had huge eyes and her ears stood out like soup-can handles. The mother had died three months previously and she was being cared for by her grandmother. Linda and Sarita and I all talked to the grandmother about immediately getting her to the hospital where I had taken Gloria, and she agreed. Sarita sent a letter to the hospital, and the child's uncle, who had a car, would drive the child to San Juan Sacatepéquez. I was relieved that I didn't have to do another 3:30 A.M. bus trip.

The teachers were still out on strike, and I used the time that I would have been in school working on lesson plans and talks for the health center.

Checking my garden, I was pleased to see the carrots were up, the chard six inches high, and the beans I had planted only four days before had sprouted. Even my melons were leafed out.

A VOLUNTEER IN THE Appropriate Technology program told me I could bake on my three-burner portable gas stove by using a large covered pot directly on the burners. I used several tuna cans for a rack under my cake pan and turned out a successful carrot cake. That evening the church across the street was having a song fest accompanied by guitar and accordion. It sounded very melodic with "swing time," but I never knew "*How Dry I Am*" was a hymn!

There was a new member in our household. When I returned from my week of Spanish, there was an indigenous woman helping in the store and in the kitchen. I'm afraid we took an instant dislike to each other. Her name was Marielena, but I never thought of her as anything but "Goody-Two-Shoes." I could handle her self-satisfied little smirk, her holier-than-thou attitude, and the problems she had making change for the pop I bought, if only she had been friendly.

Goody-Two-Shoes worked long hours. The only time I saw her sit down was in church or to eat. She was extremely religious, her only recreation being going to church. The most annoying thing was her non-stop radio which she played at full volume from 5:00 A.M. until she left for church in the evening. Evangelical radio ranged from talk shows to sermons and lots of hymns. I resented being awakened at 5:00 when I had no reason to get up. I tried hard not to antagonize her, and I was sure she believed me to be

Nap time

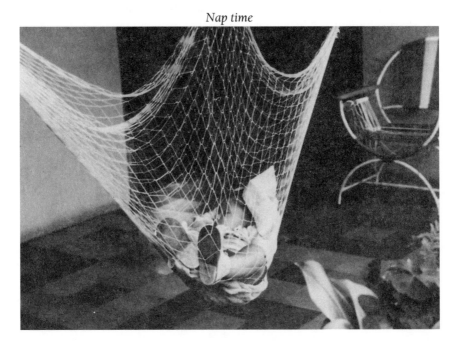

a lazy woman when she learned I didn't work at the puesto on Saturdays. She was not from Llano Grande; I don't know where Chusita found her.

The following week, Chusita left to visit her son working near Washington, D.C. I wrote as many letters as possible for her to mail there, since the postal strike was still on, and offered to let her use one of my suitcases, which pleased her.

We had a full house. Moses, Chusita's husband, was there, as well as Moses Jr., their oldest son, and his attractive wife, Lily, and their baby boy, often found sleeping in a hammock. With such a crowd, there was not enough water to wash my hair or clothes.

My son Jim sent me a package of sweet corn. I dug up a corn patch, and since every family grows some field corn, I expected mine to do well. When I asked Alicia how to say, "The seeds have sprouted" in Spanish, she said, "You say, they are born."

Several days later, I learned that Linda and Alfonso had a little boy staying with them. Assuming he was visiting, I asked how long he would be there. Linda explained that he was her husband's nephew and as neither of his parents wanted him, he would be with them until he grew up. She said he was a *regala* (gift).

Carlito was a handsome child with curls and a big smile. He had apparently been well cared for by his paternal grandparents. He had a strong body and was well nourished. We quickly became friends and I told him to call me Margarita. His new parents weren't exactly sure of his age, but guessed he was a little over three. He was a regala to me as well, for I viewed him as my Guatemalan grandson!

As I was working at my desk on a talk for midwives on "Nutrition during Pregnancy," Carlito, who was well behaved and generally no trouble, was put in bed for a nap. Linda and Alfonso slept in a room in the back of the puesto where they shared a double bed draped with mosquito netting. He called Linda for about five minutes, hoping she would let him get up. After no response, he hopefully began calling, "Margarita!" before he finally fell asleep.

ONE DAY I DREW A LARGE POSTER for the wall at the puesto showing a sad, emaciated child. Underneath, it said, "DIARRHEA CAUSES MALNUTRITION; MALNUTRITION CAUSES DIARRHEA."

Deaths from diarrhea can be prevented when a child is given sips of drinking water mixed with salt, sugar, lemon juice and baking soda. While it would make sense to have the water boiled and cooled, we told mothers to use water they drank, for fear they would not give the child anything. Baking soda is desirable for restoring electrolytes, but it isn't in every kitchen.

One of the young mothers present at my charla was named Rosa, who brought her two-year-old along. Besides being grossly fat with triple chins, he was the ugliest boy I had ever seen. His name was Nixon.

As there seemed to be no calendar noting Guatemalan holidays, I was constantly surprised by days when no one showed up for work. One day commemorated soldiers. There was still no school or any mail. I washed my sheets by hand, using the water afterwards on my garden. The Swiss chard was nearly ready to eat.

On Saturday, Barbara and I had breakfast together in Jalapa and were joined by Don Billet, who had shown me where to shop when I first came. Peace Corps news and gossip traveled faster than if it were broadcast on the radio. Barbara had heard from Kelly, her 4-H teammate, that two of the men in our training group had been sent home. The story was that they had been involved in a brawl at a town near Jalapa with some known cattle rustlers. They had all been drinking heavily when one of the cowboys shot the volunteer in the shoulder. The bullet went in and came out the other side, and the young man was sent to Washington, D.C., for medical care, along with his friend. They were told to leave the Peace Corps because of bad judgment. Both volunteers were in agricultural programs and I didn't know them well.

Another person asked to leave was a woman in her early fifties. She was a heavy smoker, recently returned from Washington where she had been treated for pneumonia. She had been told to stop smoking and was either unable or unwilling to do so. The Peace Corps maintained she was accountable for her health and not behaving responsibly.

Before I headed home that day I did my weekly marketing. I bought a papaya, baby beans, oranges for juice, mandarins, zucchini, tomatoes, lettuce and plums. At the flower stall I purchased yellow snapdragons, statice, and pink and yellow chrysanthemums.

LINDA AND I SPENT A DAY up at Carmen, an aldea two and a half kilometers straight up a hill. Her purpose was to look for children to vaccinate, but I was eager to talk to Petronia, a woman near my age. I hoped to begin my first women's group.

93

All of the homes were constructed of adobe brick with tile roofs. There were wooden frames for roof supports, windows and doors. Most of the floors were hard-packed dirt and the walls smoothly plastered with mud. Nearly everything was handmade, such as wooden chairs, benches, and tables. On the walls in the main room were diplomas, wedding pictures, and advertising calendars, some quite suggestive. The kitchen was a windowless room on the other side of the patio and contained an adobe stove. The cooking top was a waist-high counter with a hole for the fire. Some pots were ceramic and placed directly in the coals and some were metal wedged with rocks to fit in the hole. Tortillas were cooked on a *comal*, a sort of griddle of either metal or ceramic. Most families had a food grinder used for mashing black beans, an everyday staple in Guatemala. Irons were either heated on the comal or filled with hot coals.

On Petronia's dining room table was a jar filled with roses, dahlias, and lilies. Every house had a hammock on the patio, but I seldom saw a woman using it. It was a wonderful place to read, I found.

At both Carmen and Rinconada, where there was no electricity, a few families had television which they ran off their truck batteries. None of the homes had running water, so the water for drinking was collected in jugs from a community faucet; the river was used for both bathing and washing clothes.

The bus went to Rinconada twice a day, but everything had to be carried up the hill to Carmen. I felt particularly sorry for mothers of sick children having to carry them to the puesto. Occasionally, children were brought by horse from small settlements back in the hills.

ONE DAY LINDA AND SARITA worked on reports; apparently, there was paper work demanded from them as well. I spent my time making a Chutes and Ladders health game. At the roll of the dice, the player got his instructions—such as, you have boiled the water—which gets you up the ladder. Using water from the river would be some steps down. I put it on the wall for the women to play while they waited to see the doctor or the nurse. Everyone loved to play games, and I looked up the word for dice in my Spanish dictionary and hoped I could find some in Jalapa.

In the afternoon all the men and women health promoters gathered. Someone brought in a one-month-old baby who Sarita examined to show how to recognize a healthy newborn. All the participants practiced both taking temperatures, which were in centigrade, and measuring blood pressure.

July 1989

Fourth of July was a holiday and party for all the volunteers. Usually the party was held at the United States Marine House, but for some reason that year's celebration took place at a sports' complex outside of the capital. Barbara was waiting for me.

Lunch was chili, vegetarian or meat, salad, bread, pop, beer, watermelon and cookies. It was fun to see everyone, and quite a few of the Peace Corps staff were there. I bought a colorful embroidered wall hanging depicting Guatemalan life, which had been made as a 4-H project.

Afterwards, in the capital, Barbara and I shopped at the underground market which sold food and produce as well as local crafts. I bought a carved wooden crèche scene which Unitarian Barbara said she wouldn't have in her house, but I had always wanted one.

RETURNING HOME FROM JALAPA there was a different bus and driver and no Chema. They told me the old bus was *muerto* (dead).

At another meeting of the health workers and midwives, as usual no one came on time, which gave me nearly an hour to talk about nutrition and play lotteria. Sarita demonstrated how to treat wounds and administer anesthetics, letting the students practice doing sutures on a piece of meat.

Afterwards, Linda gave me the meat for Chusita's cat. Most of it I gave to Dobie, the dog, even though it was definitely "off." I then shut the cat in the room with the toilet so that the dog wouldn't eat the cat's share. It was most likely the first time the *gato's* (cat's) stomach had been full.

At the market I found chanterelle mushrooms, a rare treat. They would have to have come from the mountains. In the Pacific Northwest they are the choicest one can find, coming in the fall after rain and some warm weather. I sautéed them, adding them to scrambled eggs with which I had sliced tomatoes, the first chard from my garden, and watermelon. I hoped I could buy more as they make superb spaghetti sauce.

I should have believed Linda, for when I told her I wanted to start a women's group at 10:00 in the morning she said no one would come then. I walked up the hill to Petronia's house and she told me it was too early. One woman dropped by but went on to a neighbor's. We decided I would come back the next Monday at 2:00 in the afternoon, and she indicated her friends would love to learn to knit.

LINDA AND I SET OFF ONE MORNING for an aldea called Lás Palmas to vaccinate and check on several children. We walked along the irrigation ditch. The tobacco on one side was eight inches high and the corn on the opposite as tall, as it had begun to tassel into a beautiful copper red. We crawled under a barbed wire fence and proceeded through a herd of cows.

We found Louisa, a very thin young woman who had given birth to twins seven months before. One had died and the remaining child was lying apathetically on the dirt floor. The mother brought him to me. From looking at him I could tell something was wrong, and when we weighed him he was only seven pounds. Louisa said he was getting four spoonfuls of dry milk in his bottle. Reading the directions on the can, I told her that he should be getting seven spoonfuls at his age. He was ready for solid foods as well—mashed banana, diluted orange juice, strained carrots, egg yolks and Incaparina. I stressed he should be fed only one new food at a time and after a few days if he hadn't diarrhea or a rash she could try another food. The little waif could scarcely raise his head. Most babies at seven months are sitting up well.

On another day in handing out CARE products, Paulina came with Erika and her three older children. I recorded in the book that at two years of age Erika weighed twelve pounds. I weighed a six-year-old who had a bad case of impetigo and was definitely in the "red zone" at twenty-seven pounds. After talking to the mother about nutritious meals, I carefully wrote out two pages of ideas for foods such as *atols*, wholesome drinks made from soy powder and fruit or cereal. Linda gave the child penicillin for the impetigo, and after they left told me the mother could not read. So much for my carefully written Spanish advice!

I MET BARBARA the next day in Jalapa. As usual, she bought yarn for her 4-H girls' projects. We both purchased large plastic tubs. She had a working shower at their place, although water was not heated. I planned to use mine for a bathtub and heat water on my stove.

On the street we met a gringo who identified himself as a Canadian Mennonite missionary and invited us to drop by for a visit. We found the house with no trouble, knocked on the door and introduced ourselves to a plain woman wearing no makeup and a black cap over her bun on the back of her head. There were four children, the two little girls looking as though they lived in "The Little House on the Prairie" with their long dresses and braids. The oldest shyly offered each of us Chiclets. The mother insisted we stay for lemonade and cookies. She told us they had only been in Guatemala for four months and prior to that worked with refugees on the Mexican border. Her husband, who had been talking to a young man, joined us and said he was equipped to put in water systems and would like to cooperate with Peace Corps. We told him where he could get in touch with June and Barry, the married couple in Jalapa, as that was their expertise.

PERSPIRATION TRICKLED DOWN my face as I climbed the steep road to Carmen. The sun at midday is always the most intense, and I noticed the few women I met carried parasols or wore wide-brimmed hats. Passing a group of road workers, I said, "*Buenos tardes,*" and two young men said something I couldn't understand, which was probably just as well as several of them laughed.

It was cool on Petronia's veranda. A young woman sat on a bench nursing her baby. Nixon's cousin with the same light eyes and round head wore a ruffled dress and red anklets. She was a sturdy child, but not grossly fat like Nixon. I was beginning to wonder if more women would come when two more emerged from the house and introduced themselves as Wilma and Esperanza. I sent a woman without a baby to the neighbors to see if more were coming, and an hour later there were seven participants, all with nursing babies.

I explained I was a Peace Corps volunteer from the United States and was there to teach about health and nutrition. I mixed some Incaparina cookies from sugar, flour, oil, cinnamon and water, which we rolled into little patties and fried on the comal. Petronia's kitchen was immaculate. We passed the cookies around and each mother and child took one. When I passed them a second time I mentioned that beans and corn tortillas were good foods but to stay healthy we needed to eat a variety of foods including fruits and vegetables.

We played six games of Nutrition Lotteria. I remembered one of my Spanish texts said lottery had been a way of life since Roman times. The women would have liked to play longer, but we made plans to meet the following Monday. I noticed Petronia picked up the concept of the three food groups instantly.

Sarita, our doctor, would soon finish her public health training in Llano Grande, and I cooked a farewell lunch. We had oatmeal raisin bread—baked in my improvised oven—chicken, pineapple, cucumber, peanut salad in lettuce leaves, juice and key lime pie. I told the women it was a North American lunch and they ate it all, although Linda later told me that she didn't care for the salad.

I TOOK A BUS TO BARBARA'S, using a different route to see if it saved time. She and a new volunteer met me as the bus pulled in. A good Scandinavian cook, Barbara fixed chicken and dumplings and sautéed red and green peppers. Both were delicious. I contributed cookies and a bottle of champagne that tasted like apple juice.

There was to have been a coronation of the Queen of Matequescuintla that evening scheduled for 8:00 P.M. that hadn't begun by 10:00. We decided to go home and go to bed. The next afternoon we saw the queen and three princesses in a parade. There were to be four, but one dropped out when she found she was not chosen queen.

IT WAS A NEW WEEK and a busy Monday. I talked to a fifteen-year-old pregnant girl about nutrition, explaining that she herself was still growing and to bear a healthy child it was imperative that she eat enough food as well as a variety of foods.

That afternoon, after trudging up to Carmen, there were eight women and three men waiting for me at Petronia's house, in addition to as many babies and toddlers. We all chopped onions and tomatoes to add to cooked bulgar wheat which we served on tortillas. The men had heard how much fun their wives had had playing lotteria; they wanted to play too.

Petronia's grandson, Nixon, was there with his mother. I hoped the new doctor who was replacing Sarita could shed some light on Nixon's problem. I had diagnosed him as having every nutritional disease I had ever heard of. His face and stomach were grossly fat, but his arms and legs were normal. He had no expression on his face and I had never seen him smile, only cry. Perhaps he was retarded or had Down's syndrome. Generally he wore only a dirty T-shirt, but when I asked Rosa if I could take his picture she whisked him inside. In a short time he appeared with his hair combed and wearing a clean shirt and shorts.

ARRIVING HOME, I met the traveling brush man. Attached to his bicycle was a cart with all sorts of brooms and brushes. For a dollar I bought a long-handled broom to brush down the cobwebs and spiders in my room, a brush, and a plastic dust pan. There were rat or mouse droppings on my shelves, and I bought some Decon from Chusita.

I did wish Linda would clue me in on when things would really start. At a meeting at the puesto that was to have begun at 8:00, we waited two hours for everyone to come. In the meantime we played Chutes and Ladders with the new dice I had bought, and I read them stories in Spanish from a health book called *Between Mother and Child*.

Sarita talked to the participants about pregnancy and delivery. When she handed out hypodermic needles to everyone to practice giving each other shots, I went home for lunch.

Every volunteer is given a copy of *Where There Is No Doctor*, which is a very practical guide for surviving in the case of being away from any medical help. There were pictures of someone's arm which had been given an injection improperly, showing an ugly infection. I wanted no part of it as I wasn't sure I understood everything Sarita said, and furthermore, I didn't want to be poked by a beginner.

When I returned to the health center, they had finished with the injections. Someone brought a pan of hot tamales. Sarita's mother had sent a basket of sandwiches and Linda made a pot of hot chocolate.

There was a tearful ceremony as Sarita handed out certificates (Guatemalans love diplomas), and we all hugged her and said our good-byes.

THE FOLLOWING WEEKEND the bus was again out of order, and I had planned to go to the capital to buy tickets for a vacation trip. Alicia assured me I would get a ride to the highway and not have to walk the whole three kilometers. It had rained all night, and I rolled up my white pants to avoid being splattered with mud. After walking fifteen minutes, a young man in a pickup offered me a ride.

Steve, my oldest son; his wife, Claudia; Tarmie, eight; and Sahalie, five, would be coming for two weeks in the middle of August. I had applied for a vacation and permission to leave the country, as we planned to fly to Costa Rica the second week. Trying to get tickets on Mexican Airlines, I was told they took neither a Master Card nor a Visa, which I had, but would take American Express or cash, neither of which I had. I had hoped to have secured the reservations and tickets.

THE NEXT DAY BARBARA met me in order to go to the Biotopo Nature Preserve. I had heard about this national park ever since I had been in Guatemala, as it was one of the places where we could see resplendent quetzal birds. The royal Mayans valued them as prized possessions and only rulers wore their feathers. I had seen one only once before in a rain forest in Costa Rica.

The quetzal is dove-size with iridescent green plumage and a white breast marked with a red spot. It has a sweet, fuzzy face, but the outstanding feature is the male's long tail feathers that float behind when he flies. The bird cannot live in captivity and is a symbol of freedom. Although it is the name of the country's currency, it also is used by the Boy Scouts when one attains the highest rank in scouting. He is a quetzal scout.

After four hours on the bus, we got off on the highway and made our way to an A-frame pensión which adjoined the park with huge trees, waterfalls, and tree ferns. We thought we were taking a short walk but found ourselves climbing to the top of a high hill in dense jungle. We saw and heard birds, but no quetzals.

The rain began as we made our descent. It rains a lot in the Pacific Northwest, but nothing like a tropical downpour. I had brought a jacket, but Barbara was wet and chilled.

Because of the cool mountain climate, hypothermia can be a threat in many places in Guatemala. As we warmed up over a pot of hot tea at the comedor, we realized we had put ourselves in a foolish position. It was at least two kilometers down the steep, slippery, rock hill and we were totally alone. If one or both of us had slipped and fallen, it would have been difficult to have gotten help.

After a dinner of chicken, rice and beans, there was nothing to do but go to bed. The upstairs of the A-frame was one big room which we shared with a young English boy. After getting into bed we were so cold we pushed our beds together and pooled our blankets.

In hopes of seeing quetzals, we were up by 6:00. Some young people had just seen several females before we came out, but we were not so lucky.

W E WAITED ON THE HIGHWAY for half an hour before a bus came to take us to the coffee country around Cobán. The terrain was fairly high and the vegetation luxuriant. Prior to WWII a number of Germans owned and operated coffee plantations (fincas) there. Those flying the German flag were expelled and their property nationalized. A number became citizens; some had married Guatemalans. There is still a large German population in the capital, and in the better stores are German sausages, cheeses and bakery goods. We found a beautiful *posada*, now a hotel, that had been a lavish home. The dining room was located around a patio planted with ferns, vines, hibiscus and bougainvillea. We would have liked to have stayed there, but they were full. A teacher from New York told us there was a festival that night recognizing women from the different Mayan groups.

Wandering through the Cobán market, I bought a beautiful eight-yard hand-woven skirt for about ten dollars, and we ran into Stephanie, one of the dietitians from my training group. Over lunch, she told us her site was about three hours away where she worked at a small hospital for malnourished children. She was terribly discouraged with what she found. The doctor was a Mexican psychiatrist who had a drinking problem, and the staff cared little about the children. They were not fed suitable foods and neither the nurses nor aides fed them when they needed help. They were given tablespoons that did not fit in their mouths.

Cobán was a more sophisticated city than Jalapa. The indigenous women wore hand-woven skirts and elaborate embroidered aprons. Many wore stunning silver necklaces. The city was cleaner than Jalapa. Besides money from coffee, the region was famous for cardamom, a spice used in German and Scandinavian cooking, which in the States is expensive.

The stadium was on the edge of town, and we saw a number of Peace Corps volunteers. The Mayan girls walked down a long ramp wearing the costumes of their particular group. On the stage they gave a short speech both in Spanish and their Mayan tongue. We understood there are twenty-six distinct languages, twenty-three of which are spoken in Guatemala. It was a wonderful way to recognize the indigenous cultures that had flourished before the time of Christ until they were crushed by the conquest.

Back at Llano Grande I spent a morning working on a talk about parasites, and in the afternoon our women's group met up at Petronia's house. We prepared banana, Incaparina pancakes on which we spread fresh pineapple jam. I had to take care not to step on the baby chicks and tiny kittens that were underfoot in the kitchen that day.

Dinner was a pizza topped with Protemas, the soy meat substitute, fresh tomatoes and Edam cheese which I had bought in the capital. Goody-Two-Shoes turned up her usual gospel program as high as the volume would go, and I shut my door and played Tchaikovsky and St. Saens.

Later, when she and Alicia had gone to church, something strange occurred. Several young boys knocked on the side door, which was always kept locked, and asked for Cristobal. I did not know where he was and told them so. He appeared shortly afterward, and they all went to his room that was located on the far side of the compound around the corner. The next morning there was a boy still there who was washing his face at the pila. I could only draw conclusions. I would be glad when Chusita returned.

There was a rat in a trap Alicia had set in the dining room, and Gato, the cat, had a meal. I had noticed an alarming number of cockroaches in the buffet where the silver and dishes were stored and killed two big ones with spray.

In the heat of the day I didn't mind pouring cold water over myself for a shower, but at 6:30 I heated water for a bath in my new tub. After a breakfast of French toast, I had time to study Spanish for forty-five minutes before Goody-Two-Shoes turned on her radio.

I NEEDED TO GO TO JALAPA in order to get prices for a survey. All volunteers were required to fill out a questionnaire on how much we had to pay for seventy-five food items in order for the Peace Corps office to determine our cost-of-living allowance. It seemed like a lot of work.

Before I caught the bus back, I bought some butter, yellow button chrysanthemums and a bag of oranges. The vendor had trouble making change from the five-quetzal note I gave him. When a crowd gathered to see what the commotion was about, I showed them my arithmetic and they all agreed I was correct. This had not ever happened to me before, as most salesmen were accurate about making change.

I ran into June and we bought Cokes to take to Michelle's house, another volunteer living in Jalapa. June said she was being hassled by a man she had worked with who made it plain he would like to have an affair. I suggested she let Barry, her husband, handle the situation as Guatemala is such a male-dominated country.

Sunday morning I washed clothes. With my new plastic tub it was easy to soak them overnight with detergent and then rinse in the morning. Unless we were in the rainy season, clothes dried on the line in several hours.

As usual, church was two hours. We stood in a circle in front of the altar to receive communion. The fact that the communion wine was grape Kool-Aid didn't bother me, but the actuality of unboiled water was disturbing.

Our new doctor, named Servet, was busy brushing away cobwebs at the puesto when I arrived. He said his home was in Guatemala City and he planned to specialize in pediatrics. Nixon's mother brought in her youngest son who was terribly thin with red-rimmed eyes. I thought Servet seemed very professional and was good with him.

There was enough water in the metal barrel at the puesto so that I could wash my hair before I went home. We were practically out of water.

103

I offered Servet my room when I would be away for two weeks, but he said he had a place to stay.

In AUGUST I MET MY FAMILY at the airport. It was good to see them. Claudia brought me some blouses, a skirt, and a dress ordered from the L. L. Bean catalog, along with a nylon gym bag to use instead of my back pack. Best of all were stacks of letters.

Because streets were barricaded due to a bomb threat, we were told to stay out of the capital and took a bus to Antigua the next day. We stayed at a pensión called "Cheap Rooms" and Claudia bristled when the owner asked if the children would be "tranquil." I quickly assured him they would.

We explored the ruins of an old convent where girls from Spain had been sent to be educated. There remained fountains in the courtyards, balconies, and flowering shrubs and trees. The lower floor was a sad place reserved for the "demented" nuns.

One day we took a bus up toward a volcano where there was an indigenous town and then walked back to Antigua. At the central park Indians displayed their crafts. Claudia bought woven bags. Steve and I ran into Stephanie, the dietitian, and her sister who was visiting. She had a funny story to tell. Several weeks before, she looked across the road to see her neighbor being chased by a man with a machete. She said she sprinted as fast as she could, said a four-letter word, and snatched the machete away from the pursuer. The town gave her a new name, *Ramba*.

On Lake Atitlán we stayed at a town called Panajachel in a cabin close to the lake. It began to rain. I had been told that from mid-August through September this was to be expected, but I wasn't prepared for so much. We had all brought raincoats, but the children had wet socks most of the time.

We caught a boat that sailed across the lake to several Mayan towns. The area had been off limits as there had been guerrilla activity there. Women and girls wore cartwheel hats made from one-inch strips of woven fabric. By winding their long hair in the strips, the hat stayed on. Sahale was a friendly five-year-old and would have liked to have played with some of the children. Unfortunately, we could not speak their language. Later at a restaurant, a little Indian girl about Sahale's age joined us. My granddaughter was coloring with crayons in a Spanish coloring book. The child spoke her Mayan dialect, but it didn't stop her from coloring with

Sahale or sharing our lunch, both of which we encouraged. She must have been hungry as she ate as many sandwiches as Tarm and his sister together.

We hunted all over the town of Panajachel for a laundromat. Tarm had the dirtiest socks I had ever seen, and as we dumped our clothes in the pila to wash them, the owner's wife took over and with much scrubbing and bleaching got them clean. As it was raining, we weren't able to dry the clothes, and we carried them wet to Costa Rica the next day where they dried in our hotel room.

The week was filled with walks on sunny beaches, a trip to the rain forest where we all saw the elusive quetzal as well as toucans, bell birds and a toucanet. We sadly said good-bye at the airport when Steve and his family left for New England. I didn't see them again for nearly two years.

Sahale and the Mayan children

Marge's grandchildren,
Sahale and Tarm

105

September 1989

On my way home I stopped at the market in Jalapa where I bought smoked pork chops, lean hamburger (there is never excess fat on the beef), apples to bake, peppers to stuff, and two lovely bunches of pink and red-orange zinnias. On my table there was a pile of mail. The postal strike was over.

The school strike was settled as well. I taught three classes and was nervous, but needn't have been. That night the power was off. Fortunately, I could listen to shortwave when I couldn't see to knit, read, or work on my quilt.

Eloisa, the minister's wife, came over with a sweater she had ripped out and was having me help her re-knit. She and Pablo said I would be able to use the church to show health and nutrition movies. The poor woman was only in her early thirties and had just lost her upper two front teeth.

There was a meeting again of health workers and midwives at the puesto where I did a talk on parasites. I made a chart on which I drew some ugly looking worms, and Servet reinforced what I had said. He took himself rather seriously, but was very thorough. He would do as well as Sarita, I thought.

Friday was another unexplained holiday for the health center that gave me a chance to work at home before catching the 1:30 bus for Jalapa. Barbara had a meeting with the agricultural people.

It was fun sharing my Costa Rica trip with her. June and Barry invited us over for dinner, and she served us bacon carbonado, pan leche (rolls made with milk from a new bakery), and a vegetable salad. Barbara brought a bottle of champagne and I brought apples and made an apple crisp.

At home I was able to store vegetables and meat in the refrigerator and put other foods high on a shelf in my room. The miserable cat ate my rolls from the good bakery.

Chusita was back and brought me a Mounds bar, which I told her was my favorite. She had bought an enormous picture of two tigers gamboling in the snow, which hung slightly askew over the couch on the patio.

It was a good thing she was back, as Dobie needed first aid. He was in a terrible dog fight again and had bites all over, with a particularly wicked gash over his eye. One claw had been nearly torn off and he limped pitifully on three legs. Chusita gave him a bath through which he was calm and patient. I noticed he was tied up for the next several days.

I needed some first aid as well, as there was so much wax in my ears I was having trouble hearing. Barbara waited in the Peace Corps office for me while the nurse cleaned out my ears. Afterwards we took a bus to see a famous relief map of Guatemala which was constructed in a park. The map was 2500 square meters and was viewed from above on a platform. The mountains were clearly shown so that the vertical scale was twice that of the horizontal. There was running water in the rivers, but the remarkable feature was that the map was completed in 1905.

On the university campus there is a lovely botanical park I had visited before, but as usual, it was closed. A block away is an interesting pink church built as a chapel. The cross on top is tilted, we assumed the result of an earthquake.

BARBARA REPORTED AN UNPLEASANT experience of her 4-H partner, Kelly, up at Mateque. He and three other volunteers, two of them women, were standing in front of his house when a very drunk man ran up to them and began shooting. Unfortunately, his house was locked and they ran around the corner, the man following and shouting, "Gimme a cigarette, gringo." Kelly turned face-to-face with the drunk, and he and the other male volunteer wrestled the gun away from him. After the man ran off, they reported the event to the police, but they were told there needed to be three witnesses, all Guatemalans. Kelly was so shaken up he spent the week in the capital and asked to go to Washington for counseling, which was denied. He was requesting another site.

LIESL, FROM THE NEW nutrition group, was assigned to Mateque and rented a house six miles from town up in the hills, where she was surrounded by coffee trees. She was offered a huge undisciplined dog owned by one of the trainers, who was the mother of two little boys as unruly as the dog. Chok, named after the Mayan rain god, was probably cute when he was a puppy jumping into people's laps, but at over 100 pounds, none of us were thrilled.

It took three buses for Liesl to get Chok from Antigua to her house, along with a 100-pound bag of dog food. No diet of dried tortillas for him. Chok loved his new home. To accommodate him, she moved all her belongings off tables and counters, for he knocked off dishes, clothes, food and books when he wagged his tail. He happily attended school, the health center, or club meetings whenever Liesl went for her nutrition duties.

There was a problem, however, when the dog discovered chickens, and the neighbors did not take kindly to eight of theirs being killed. It took a third of Liesl's monthly salary to replace them.

Chok was put on a leash while Liesl walked to work, but he was so strong she was pulled along like a toy on a string. After he managed to kill more chickens in town, she decided he would have to be returned to his original owner. With every trip to town, she brought down ten pounds of dog food to try to sell to some dog owner who might be willing to buy food for his pet.

At last, the day came for Chok to return home. He happily jumped on the bus and slid under the seat. The ride to Guate took four hours, and after about ten minutes Liesl's seat mate began to sniff. The people in front of her turned around, wrinkling their noses, and it was then, much to her horror, she discovered that Chok had diarrhea. The bus as usual was crowded, they were in the middle of nowhere, and there was no question of getting off. She cleaned up the mess as best she could, but the four hours seemed interminable. After leaving the country bus, there was a city bus to catch and then the Antigua bus for another hour's ride.

How delighted the first owners were, we never heard, but eventually Chok became a hero. His third owner was a well-to-do family living in the suburbs where Chok had a job guarding the house. When *ladrones* (robbers) scaled the wall topped with broken glass, the dog bravely defended the new home. He was badly knifed, bleeding and barely alive when the owners returned. The thieves fled without their loot, and Chok was rushed to the vet for a dog-to-dog transfusion. The namesake of the rain god lived, and everyone said, "Thank God for Chok."

WHEN LINDA ASKED ME to go up to Rinconada

108

with her, I was glad to go as I wanted to see a woman named Macaria about starting a women's group at her house. It had rained so much we took off our shoes to cross the river which nearly covered the rocks we generally used for stepping stones. Walking up the hill, she said to me, "Margarita, I'm having a baby in March and I plan to call her Margarita." I was both touched and thrilled. I had thought she seemed a bit testy, which was not her usual temperament. I had never had a namesake and I gave her a big hug.

We proceeded down the hill together and back across the river where I continued on up to Carmen. I taught a class at the school there on nutrition and then sat in the shade and ate my lunch of a tuna sandwich, an apple, and lemonade I had frozen in a plastic bottle.

When I walked over to Petronia's house for our women's "reunion," her husband was standing on the porch shaving with a double-edged razor blade that he held between two fingers. I imagined that to be a difficult feat. Razor blades were called *gilletes*.

In attempting to make pancakes on an adobe stove, I did the worst food demonstration in my teaching experience. Generally, I brought all necessary utensils, but it never occurred to me Petronia would have neither a frying pan nor a pancake turner. Using a sauce pan with a stick was not satisfactory. My talk on vitamin A went well from my point of view, and I attempted to teach five girls how to knit.

Marge and Linda at the health center

109

October 1989

Guatemala's Independence Day in October meant a three-day holiday. I met Barbara at the old train station in downtown Guate where we took a Pullman bus on our way to ruins in Honduras called Copán. Like the Petén farther north and the lowlands on the coast, the weather was hot, humid and steamy. We rode to a large city called Chiquimula and from there took a bus to the border. There was no problem clearing customs and riding in a truck to the town. We were surprised to be in a lush green area of clean rivers and large shade trees. Copán was cleaner than most Guatemalan towns, and we were lucky to find a pensión, where we got the last room. The beds and bedding were superior to what we had had in Guatemala at anything but the best hotels and that night we slept like logs.

The walk to the ruins was a kilometer, and although the area was not as large as either Tikal or Chichén Itzá in Mexico, the setting was lovely. The grass was mowed, possibly because of snakes, with a huge expanse of green and three-hundred-year-old trees. On several sides were pyramids constructed on stone blocks. Histories of various kings and noteworthy dates were carved on stone steles which resembled tombstones. There was the usual Mayan ball court where games were played, in which it is thought the losers were beheaded.

Hearing someone calling our names, we looked to the top of one of the pyramids to see Todd, the assistant Peace Corps director. Strictly speaking, we shouldn't have been there as we hadn't gotten permission for leaving Guatemala; however, it wasn't mentioned when Todd gave us a lift back to our motel. We wondered if Copán was like Antigua, a place where tourists went that was not representative of the rest of the country.

We had trouble getting a mini-bus back to the border, and after talking to two different drivers, neither of whom we liked the looks of, we rode in a truck. That driver said we had made a good choice as both the bus drivers had been drinking.

Going back a different route over the mountains to Jalapa, we passed through indigenous towns named Jocotán, Camotán and San Pedro Penula. The road was narrow with a steep drop on one side and no guard rails. The women wore traditional woven skirts and blouses, and the long white veils they wore on their heads reached to their knees.

Arriving in Jalapa too late for me to shop and catch my morning bus, I ran into Barry at the market. He invited me home where we spent the afternoon playing Scrabble in both Spanish and English.

The next day while I was alone in the puesto, I found I was able to read Servet's pediatrics book. It was most likely easy to read as it had been translated from English. I decided then that Nixon had kwashiorkor. His moon face, bad disposition and apathy were all symptomatic of severe protein deficiency.

I had ordered from the United States a film strip done by the March of Dimes called *Inside My Mom* about nutrition during pregnancy. Linda had me show it twice at the puesto, being able to relate to the situation. I had used it when I taught nutrition in Tacoma. The "star" was a personable fetus who expressed what he liked and didn't like about his mother's food habits. In the English version the fetus called the doctor "Old Cold Hands" which the women always thought was funny. In the Spanish tape he was called *Doctorcita*, literally "Little Doctor," a put down. I showed the film strip as well to the 4-H women and girls at their meeting.

I was asked to begin another women's group at Carmen by some women who said they didn't get along with Petronia and her relatives and neighbors or vice versa. I hoped I could arrange the meetings one after the other.

TYPICAL OF SEPTEMBER WEATHER, there was non-stop rain all day. Church was another "session" or business meeting. When I was a girl, my father was on the session in the Presbyterian church, but meetings weren't in place of Sunday services. The congregation would meet again at night.

I took dinner over to Linda's, having fixed stuffed sweet red peppers, green salad, garlic rolls, strawberry Jell-O with bananas and toll house cookies. They ate everything.

While the rain pattered on my tile roof, I listened to Voice of America and British Broadcasting as I sewed together a blue cotton sweater I had knit.

GUATEMALA PEACE CORPs put out a now-and-then newsletter called *The Id* where budding writers submitted poetry, short stories, and commentaries on serious subjects as well as on other subjects. Last summer I had sent in a recipe for oatmeal bread and suggested the last edition resembled a collection of articles from *Time*, a high school newspaper, *Harpers*, and *Mad* magazine. In the next issue they printed my recipe, but not my comment.

One day at the health center a woman with a four-month-old baby, who had a throat abnormality preventing her from swallowing normally, asked me for twenty quetzales for bus fare to go to the capital to the doctor. I gave it to her.

At the end of September everything clicked at school in Llano Grande. Again, I sat on the floor with the first graders and rolled a ball to each child who told me foods containing vitamins A and C, and we talked about iron. The other classes were all attentive, and I came away feeling I had taught them.

There was enough water in the oil drum to be able to wash clothes, although no water in the pipes. It had stopped raining and most of my clothes got dry. The sky was clear and the stars were out.

In the morning I chugged up to the school at Carmen to find there were only girls attending. Raphael, the teacher, explained that the boys were all working in the tobacco fields. I returned home, hot and perspiring, poured cold water over myself, and dressed in a white blouse with lace edging around the neck and a navy blue Guatemalan skirt with an embroidered yolk. Wearing boots, I carried my sandals to the health center as the road was gooey with mud.

I was scheduled to give a talk on vitamin A and how blindness could be prevented in very young children. There were only a handful of women, and we waited an hour and a half for seven who didn't show up.

Making a quick trip to Jalapa to a yardage store, I bought flannel for the inside of my quilt, as I had nearly finished piecing and sewing together the strips. The girls at the store knew me and had gone to school with Linda. I tried to explain what I needed and finally consulted my pocket dictionary and asked for *franela* (flannel). At the market I purchased a fly swatter called a *matamosca*, which translates to "fly killer."

THAT EVENING I WAS HOME alone with Grandma and all the doors were locked. My quilt was stretched out on the dining room table, and Eloisa called through the window to ask Grandma what she should do about five-year-old Pablito who had been sick all day. I had seldom heard her say anything and considered her pretty senile. Since *Abuelita* (little grandmother) had no answers, I gave Eloisa the thermometer from my first aid kit and said I would see if Servet was still at the puesto.

The rain came down in torrents, but I wore a rain jacket and boots and took an umbrella to run the two blocks through the mud. Servet generally went home weekends, but fortunately he was still there and came back with me carrying a stethoscope and thermometer in centigrade. Servet had him stand and try to walk, and he told me it could be meningitis as one side was affected. I stayed with Eloisa while the doctor went back for phenobarb to control convulsions, and he arranged to go to the hospital with her in the morning.

I invited Servet to come in for soup, only to find Chusita had locked the door to the farmacia where the refrigerator was located. In my room I found a package of minestrone soup to which I added a potato to make it go farther and we had garlic bread, melon and cookies.

After church the next day, Abner, Carolina and Otto came over, as their parents were still at the hospital with Pablito. The older children and I were just finishing making oatmeal cookies for their family when Eloisa came over with Pablito and reported they were going to another hospital the next day for more tests. It appeared the child did not have meningitis.

Until dark I worked on my quilt. I had planned to study, but the mosquitoes were so bad it was impossible. Since this was both a malaria and denge fever (mosquito carrying disease) area, I did my best to avoid being bitten.

113

POOR GLORIA, THE MOTHER of one of my students, came in to the puesto again with burns on the palm of her hand and fingers. This was the second time in two weeks she had suffered an epileptic seizure while making tortillas and fallen on the hot comal. Apparently, her sister was in worse shape than she and unable to do anything. Gloria's mother ran a small tienda close to the school and always gave me a hug and a whiskery kiss whenever I came by.

I had time alone at the puesto all week. Servet had gone for meetings in the capital and Linda to a two-day conference in Jalapa. It was nice to be able to work at the puesto without having to block out Goody-Two-Shoes' incessant radio programs. What I had hoped would be a productive day ended with my having a temperature of 101, along with diarrhea. All the teachers drove from Jalapa each school day, and I waited to tell Rafilia I wouldn't be coming up to Carmen and to send a child over to Petronia's house to tell her I was sick.

Several days later, I did a food demonstration at the puesto, cooking bulgar wheat and milk. It was too sweet for me, but those folks liked anything cooked with sugar.

I weighed myself and was down to 132 pounds which wasn't much more than I weighed in college. I still wasn't feeling well and went to bed after lunch.

The following day I loaded up on Lomotil and headed for Guate and the Peace Corps office. I thought I was better, but the nurse sent me to the lab with a stool sample. I wouldn't get the results for several days and needed to go to Jalapa where there was a telephone. Actually, there was a phone in the farmacia, but it hadn't functioned since I had come, and I didn't know how long before that.

In my box at the Peace Corps office there was a stack of mail, one long letter from a college friend telling me how much she worried about me. It was nice to know someone was concerned.

Barbara arrived about 5:00 in the afternoon and we had dinner at a German restaurant I had found. They served particularly good pea soup and German potato salad. Saturday was a shopping day. Barbara was always looking for yarn for her 4-H girls. I bought yarn to make a sweater for Linda's baby and at a hardware store a small Teflon pan made in Spain. We took a bus to a supermarket where I bought cheese, cocoa, yeast and some granola for Chusita. For lack of anything else to do, we went to an *Indiana Jones* movie. At our hotel Barbara cut my bangs, which were getting too long, and that night watched *Gorillas in the Mist* on the TV in our room. The hotel got CNN, which we always watched to catch up on news.

Back home Maria was handing out food sent to the Guatemalan Agriculture Department. There were cans of chicken from Holland, oil from Canada and corn from the U.S. A few people paid a little and Maria kept records of those receiving food. I brought my second quilt strip to show the girls.

CHUSITA ASKED ME to do a program at the end of November for United Church Women in Jalapa. There would be several hundred women attending and I said "Yes" because I thought I should and was flattered to be asked. However, it meant I'd miss the last day of the Peace Corps Conference taking place after Thanksgiving.

After spending the morning teaching four classes, I took the bus to Jalapa to call Kathy, the nurse at the Peace Corps office. My lab reports were negative, although I still had diarrhea. At least I wasn't host to some parasite.

I picked up some photo copying of a little leaflet I had written for the mothers at the health center on vaccinations. I wasn't too happy with the printing, but it was readable and gave the schedule for shots all children should have. I found most of the young mothers could read, but many woman my age could not.

I GOT TO BARBARA'S TOWN in record time, only five and a half hours. As the crow flies, she wasn't more that a hundred miles from me. The new route wasn't as scenic as going over the mountains, but the bus schedule meshed more conveniently. Liesl stopped by and said she would come to Llano Grande in November and in the meantime talk with our supervisor at the hospital in Jalapa about how to get a fluoride project started at our respective sites.

Saturday was a domestic day. I bought a bread board in town and baked two loaves of oatmeal bread. Barbara had found a pattern for small knitted dolls I tried out, and I did a strip on my quilt.

Elizabeth, who worked in the forestry program, came over for dinner,

and we had Bloody Mary's made with tomato juice and something unidentifiable I had bought. Barbara fixed Swedish meatballs served with mashed
potatoes and mushroom gravy. Elizabeth said she was with Kelly when he
was accosted by the drunk with the gun. At that time she was dating a
young Guatemalan whose father owned a coffee finca.

Going home I rode with a young volunteer from Philadelphia who had
been visiting Liesl. I told him that my Spanish was coming along, and that
while I could discuss health, vitamins, food, children's diseases, worms
and diarrhea, it led to a pretty one-sided conversation. Aaron replied that
he had worked for six months at a kibbutz in Israel where they raised
chickens. He had been able to discuss in detail Hebrew chicken diseases,
but added sadly that no one cared.

I HAD BEGUN TO WORK into a comfortable sched-
ule at the three schools, the puesto and my women's groups. I gave out cat
and mouse stickers, dividing the children into teams like a spelling bee
and asking nutrition questions. The second and third graders did well, the
fourth and fifth graders even better, and we all had a good time. The children were cooperative and quiet and excited over the score and the com-
petition.

The sixth grade was a different story. They were noisy when they assembled, and I told them I would leave if they did not quiet down. The
class was in an uproar, and I found myself shouting in order to be heard.
Small children were looking in the windows. They got the message when
I told them I could not teach a class that misbehaved, and I left.

After lunch I helped Linda and Irma, the janitor, bag rice and cornmeal
while we waited for twelve new health promoters to assemble. Servet was
young and handsome and the girls giggled their way through his charla on
malnutrition, to which I added information on vitamin A.

I hadn't brought my umbrella (*para agua*)—*para sol* being for the sun—
and was so wet after walking home that I crawled under my blankets to get
dry and warm.

IT TOOK THIRTY-FIVE minutes to climb the hill to
the school at Carmen. After class I sat in a patch of wild zinnias and

marigolds and ate my lunch. I was gratified that twelve women and twenty-four children showed up for my new women's group. As lunch was being served to the men, and Olellia, the housewife, was busy making tortillas, I didn't cook anything. We played lotteria, talked about the three food groups, and I showed them ideas for knitting. The women seemed a little more affluent and sophisticated than Petronia's group.

I was disappointed when I arrived at Petronia's house that only one woman was there. Eventually four more drifted in, including Nixon, his red-rim-eyed brother and Rosa, their mother. Nixon was as ugly as ever but seemed a little friendlier, and his small brother had perked up. I cooked bulgar wheat with milk and sugar, which was all slurped up.

LINDA AND CARLITO and I walked over to Terrones, the aldea below us, and visited at a few homes. When we arrived at Elinora's, the good witch doctor who prescribes green juice, she took charge of Carlito. She rubbed him all over, felt the pulse in his neck, and took him inside the house where there was an altar. I was curious to know what she was doing, and later Linda said Elinora was making the sign of the cross over him. We were served coffee with no sugar as a concession to me, fresh tortillas, beans and dry salty cheese.

We left for more calls, and as it was hot, we all drank a soda at a tienda. Much to my surprise, on the way back we stopped at Elinora's again where her daughter fixed us lunch. At breakfast, Tina was wringing the neck of a chicken, and she served the broth with macaroni, tough chicken meat, more tortillas, and coffee. It was obvious the community valued Linda, as they were very good to her.

ARNOLDO WAS A TEENAGE NEPHEW of Chusita who was often at the house and very active in the church. He was playing a religious tape in the dining room, at the same time the church across the street was broadcasting hymns over their loudspeaker, and Goody-Two-Shoes' radio was at full volume. With a big smile, Arnoldo asked me if I liked the *musica*. I flatly said, "No." I'm sure he was horrified. I didn't add that it drove me crazy.

The radio was off when Goody-Two-Shoes went to church at night, which was five nights out of seven. I finished Kurt Vonnegut's book on the Galápagos Islands I had gotten out of the Peace Corps library, as two of my sons and I were going there over Christmas. Vonnegut was not my favorite author.

THE HEALTH CENTER WAS OPEN in the morning even though it was Revolution Day, and we handed out CARE products. I had a free afternoon. I gave my room a thorough cleaning, including the top of the door and bulletin board, brushing down the walls and moving the furniture. I took everything off my floor-to-ceiling shelves, dispatching six cockroaches. Some were hiding in folded sweaters and others inside the pages of notebooks. They particularly liked corners of cardboard boxes. It was immensely satisfying to dispense with them by tossing them to the chickens who greedily swallowed them in one gulp.

One Monday Linda and I walked up to Rinconada past three houses where Linda said families refused to allow their children to be immunized. I asked her about the *ojo* (the evil eye), and she told me many people believed that was the cause of impetigo and other infections.

The mail didn't seem to be coming through again. I was notified I had a package at the post office in Monjas where Chusita picked up our mail, but she had gone to the capital.

The week went by quickly. I introduced *Maraquita Cochinita* (little pig), a story of a dirty little girl who seldom washed, ate junk food, and when she was thirsty drank from the river. The results of her health habits were good teaching tools for my classes.

At the health center I talked to the health promoters about encouraging women to breast feed. I wrote another booklet saying there is no good substitute for mother's milk and that it is perfect for human babies just as cat's milk is for kittens, and cow's milk for calves. Besides, it was the right temperature, cheaper, cleaner and more convenient.

LINDA SAID THE ELECTRIC BILL at the puesto was too high because of the hot plate I had bought to use for food demonstrations. I didn't want to give up cooking there and noticed Linda found it convenient for sterilizing needles and other equipment.

At my women's groups I shared what I had done at school and played the *Three-Food-Group* tape and a health song sung to the *Battle Hymn of the Republic*. People seemed to like any music no matter what the words were. I prepared a fruit drink with Incaparina, guavas, bananas, orange and lemon juice. Even though that family was more affluent than my other group, I was surprised there were no forks in their kitchen, only tablespoons. We played lotteria until it was time to leave for Petronia's house where I repeated the performance.

The following day I confirmed that we would have a women's group in Rinconada. I taught my last class at the school there until the next February, and started down the hill. The grandmother of the terribly malnourished child, whose uncle had taken her to the hospital where Gloria had gone, came running out of her house. Grandma was all smiles and showed me a colored picture of the little girl who was living with an aunt. The child had lots of dark hair and appeared alert and healthy. I gave Grandma a hug.

Barbara came on the noon bus on Friday and I took her over to the 4-H meeting. I had expected to cook, but the girls had brought crochet hooks and yarn and spent the afternoon making granny squares under Barbara's direction. Barbara was able to buy fruit and vegetables at her town, but I came home from Jalapa with white beans and a smoked pork chop for soup, bacon for Spanish rice, hamburger for spaghetti and apples for baking. Why I didn't gain weight with all the cooking and eating I did, I never understood.

Linda was on vacation until the middle of December. She and Carlito and Alfonso were taking the train to Livingston where his parents had a finca. Among other things they raised bananas, grapefruit and oranges. I was invited to go but felt I should stay home and work, a decision I would always regret.

With the rain, the countryside was covered with wild flowers. There were tiny maroon and lavender morning glories covering whole hillsides and a larger morning glory in the lovely shade of blue the Spanish call *celeste*. One day from the bus window I spotted pink frangi pangi and everywhere small yellow sunflowers. My area, called the oriente, just needed rain to be beautiful.

All the rivers were running swiftly, many the color of chocolate, meaning a precious top soil was being washed away.

119

On HALLOWEEN, Servet and Linda gathered the children together after dark. Carlito appeared at my door wearing a huge jacket, Alfonso's wide-brimmed hat, a necktie and mustache, looking like a small version of his uncle. Other children, dressed like witches, rattled cans and called out to the goblins and spirits. No one had introduced them to trick or treating, but I made a mental note to carve jack-o'-lanterns the next year.

All Saints' Day seemed to be like our Memorial Day and was a two-day holiday. It was windy and the boys were flying kites and the men all seemed to be at home.

I climbed up to Rinconada for my first women's group. All the women were busy making tamals, the holiday food Estella had made last Christmas, and the same thing was going on up at Carmen.

I had seen wreaths of plastic flowers in Jalapa stores. At home, Alicia was fastening paper flowers to sprays of lemon leaves to take to the cemetery situated on a hillside near Rinconada. I walked the mile up the hill to see what was going on. The drinking had not begun; people wearing their best clothes were picnicking beside family graves. On one side a soccer game was in process, and fried tortillas, filled buns and sodas were sold. The graves were decorated with fresh flowers, plastic flowers, flags and swags. Alicia said she liked to go early while the men were still sober.

I met Servet, who had ridden up on his bicycle. He said he had finally seen Nixon, and his problem was that he was just plain fat. So much for my diagnoses, but I still didn't think he was normal.

I made marmalade by slicing mandarin oranges thinly and soaking them all night in an equal amount of sugar. The next day I added the juice of a lemon and boiled the jam until it was thick. It was delicious.

There didn't seem to be much going on at the puesto. I made Linda a maternity dress with a yoke on which she embroidered flowers. For lack of anything else to do, I began knitting a big red Santa for the waiting room.

One night as I was lying in bed I saw a rat the size of a half-grown gringo kitten walk straight up my brick wall. I say "gringo kitten" because Guatemalan cats are so malnourished they are about half the size of those in the U.S. I would buy rat poison the next time I was in town.

I was up at 6:00 to bake a birthday cake for Servet. I used a box of Betty Crocker cake mix, but my stove was not completely level and the layers were tilted. Using marmalade for the filling, I made frosting from powdered sugar and orange juice. There was a crack on the top which I covered with a yellow hibiscus and it looked most festive.

THERE WERE THREE DIFFERENT women's groups that week. Petronia had malaria, but seemed to be up and about. At Olillia's we worked on knitting, which several of the women mastered instantly. The next day I took the bus to Rinconada, which made it easier for me to carry food and utensils. The women there had curious names such as Incarnation, Conception and Macaria.

LIESL AND I TRIED to see the public health dentist in Jalapa to get his help for our fluoride project, but the doctor was out and we left him a note. Together we worked on an in-service training on health and nutrition for teachers in January. We would begin in Mateque and finish in Llano Grande. Each session would be two days and we would try to include the dentist for the fluoride project.

The following day the bus was either stuck in the mud or broken, we weren't sure, so we began walking to the highway and were given a lift by a man in a pick-up. I had an appointment to have the top of my hair permed. I wore the back pinned up, but anyone who touched it wanted to braid it. I let the girl do a braid in back, but as usual found it too hot.

I heard some sad news of Connie, my young roommate the four days we were in Miami. She was very immature and had done little dating. In the first few months she became smitten with an older Guatemalan who both drank and accepted any extra money she would give him. Volunteers wanting to marry during their term of service needed the approval of the Peace Corps, and the request was denied on the grounds he was an undesirable person. She had been advised by many people not to date him, but she went through with the marriage and was expelled from the Peace Corps. When they cleared customs at the airport in Miami, he promptly disappeared.

BOTH JUNE AND BARBARA stayed with me one night. June had just finished the oven up at Rinconada with the hope that

121

the women could start a bakery. My job was to teach them how to bake bread. I hoped the oven would heat properly and asked my son Clark to bring an oven thermometer when he came at Christmas. We all cooked dinner—stuffed peppers, cole slaw with tomato dressing, lemon bars, mandarin oranges and tea.

Saturday morning, after not sleeping well because of the mosquitoes buzzing, I was rudely awakened at 4:15 by the church's loudspeaker blasting out a hymn. Later, I found it was the birthday of Pablo, the minister. He wanted the community to share it with him.

June

At 6:00, when I caught the bus on the corner, the congregation had been singing for nearly two hours and were still going strong. Our usually careful driver careened down the road faster than I had ever seen him drive. On the highway he would have rammed another bus if that driver would have let him pass. Later, he tried to pass in spite of an oncoming car that swerved at the last minute, and I was ready to get off. In Monjas, which was a half hour away, the driver got out and spent a long time at the police station. Apparently, he had been reported, as he had a wad of papers in his hand and proceeded to drive circumspectly all the way to Jalapa.

Returning home at noon, I went to bed after lunch, again being awakened by the loud hymns played over the loudspeaker. The next broadcast was a sermon and several solos, all of which lasted two more hours. The following day I mentioned to Jorge, who visited often and enjoyed reading my *Newsweek* magazines, that I found the loudspeaker annoying. He agreed, saying there was a very sick woman in the neighborhood who was disturbed by all the noise. I didn't imagine the situation made converts of any of the Catholics.

November 1989

I set the alarm the night before I left Llano Grande for the Thanksgiving festivities in the capital. It failed to go off, but fortunately the bus was late. I rode the four hours to Guate and headed for the Peace Corps office. We needed to renew our visas each year, and I picked up my passport with its new stamp. Another college friend had sent me a stack of bread recipes I could use for the bakery up at Rinconada.

When Barbara arrived, we walked up to Avenida Reforma to shop for a gift to take to our host, ending up with cheese and wine. We had directions for the Wiggens' condo but felt safer taking a cab. All volunteers were entertained in diplomats' or U.S.A.I.D. homes or at the embassy for Thanksgiving.

Besides several friends of the Wiggens, we were joined by two young men—Aaron, who could discuss chicken diseases in Hebrew, and Jeff in the forestry program. We all wore our best clothes. One of the men brought flowers and the other a bag of peanuts.

Our host had worked for U.S.A.I.D. in three African countries as well as Pakistan. After gin and tonics and paté with French bread, we had a wonderful traditional dinner. I had offered to make the gravy and my hostess accepted.

Afterwards, we were driven to the ambassador's home where Tom Strook, the new ambassador, who liked the Peace Corps, had invited us all for popcorn, beer, soft drinks and a dance band. Mrs. Strook was Cuban by birth and one of the most charming women I had ever met. She said she had met her husband when she attended Wellesley.

The palatial residence was surrounded by a huge yard for garden parties, and it even had a swimming pool and tennis courts.

The volunteer conference was held at a large hotel. Kathy, the head nurse, discussed Peace Corps evaluations on medical care that had been handed in. I thought she seemed to be on the verge of tears and would have given her a hug had I had the opportunity. Instead, I wrote her a note telling her I felt she and the staff were doing a professional job. I wondered why many young volunteers were so critical of anyone in authority.

There was a talk on environmental concerns followed by information on what could be expected from coming elections. That speaker was a former volunteer currently working for the state department. One of the young men from my training group was highly critical of his speech. Adding to the problem was that he was so bright and personable, whatever that meant.

After dinner someone showed slides, which were good enough to have been done by a professional. Barry played the guitar and sang, and other volunteers put on a dating- game skit.

BECAUSE OF MY CHURCH WOMEN'S commitment, I had to miss the second day of the conference. I wasn't scheduled to show my slides on nutrition until late in the afternoon, meaning I would miss the bus and need to spend the night in Jalapa.

The morning was taken up with a contest for women to recite Bible verses, which Eloisa won hands down. A beautiful niece of Chusita's was chairman, and besides the Llano Grande people, there were at least one-hundred-fifty women from surrounding areas. They served a lovely lunch in the churchyard. Mothers and small children had slept on the floor throughout rooms adjoining the church.

I showed my film strip, *Inside My Mom*, which was in Spanish, talked about nutrition and pregnancy, and prepared "bulgar wheat, Llano Grande" and Incaparina cookies I baked on a comal. I felt good about it all, was warmly received, and even complimented on my Spanish.

I had hoped to stay at Michelle's house, but she was still in Guatemala City at the Peace Corps Conference. I had dinner at the Chinese Chicken and ran into one of her admirers, of which she had many, named Roberto, who had spent a year at Iowa State. I knew he had dated pretty Rosemary, the teacher of Rinconada. He said he had hoped Michelle had come home and he had left a note under her door.

EACH MUNICIPALIDAD like Jalapa had A.V. equipment for volunteers to use. I had brought back a movie on family planning to show at the puesto, 4-H and church. Servet and I had trouble getting the machine to work. (I was used to equipment maintained by Tacoma schools.) But, we were finally able to roll the film.

Pablo wasn't sure a birth control film would be suitable for the children, so I gave him a preview. It was a Disney film narrated by Donald Duck speaking Spanish, and it showed a family who had so many children there was not enough food and no money for school. In another family, the wife whispered to her husband, who folded his arms and shook his head. After some persuasion and much whispering, he finally agreed. Pablo approved, and when we showed it to the congregation, they liked it so well they saw it three times!

Another night Servet and I showed health movies in the sanctuary. Some of the children had never seen a *pelicula* (movie). *Hungry Angels* had been filmed in Guatemala and concerned three women who gave birth at the same time, and because of circumstances due to ignorance and poverty nearly lost them. I used to show the film at home, and the last scenes were taken at the children's hospital where Gloria had been taken. The audience was two-thirds children and the church was packed. Many of the children thought the emaciated bodies and gaunt looks of babies were funny, and the doctor and I explained if the infants had had proper food and their vaccinations they would not have been sick. Donald Duck again narrated some cartoons on malaria and diarrhea, which everyone enjoyed.

CHUSITA HAD JUST RETURNED from the capital and reported that the city bus drivers there were on strike. Taxi drivers did a thriving business, I was sure.

Petronia was in the health center for the malaria. Gloria, the woman with the burns on her hands, came in and gave me a hug and kiss, as her mother generally did. She told me her husband had gone to the United States and never returned. A very thin man I hadn't seen before was coughing badly, and Servet did a sputum test for tuberculosis.

I ran in to Jalapa to take care of my laundry and shopping and brought sweet rolls over to Michelle's house where we had them with coffee. Michelle reported that she and June and Barry and Christene, a nurse nearby, all had amoebas (parasites causing diarrhea). It was probably just as well I hadn't stayed at the conference for the last day.

I asked her about Roberto, and she said she had told him to get lost. She had a new boyfriend from El Salvador who played on a soccer team, and she planned to take him home with her for Christmas. She had decided to get a job in Jalapa after Peace Corps.

IN MARINA'S KITCHEN I scrubbed the table before I kneaded the bread. While it was rising, Kelly, Erica, and several other little girls walked to Macaria's house for a women's meeting. The girls were fun. I saw them both at school and 4-H. We held hands as we walked and sang songs, and I taught them some English words. Kelly was sure she would want to live in the United States when she grew up.

Back at Marina's house the bread turned out beautifully—two loaves of golden whole wheat. I hoped the women would make a go of their community bakery.

Marina lived in a brick house, and they owned a truck with Connecticut license plates as her husband worked at times in the U.S. When I asked where their latrine was, they said they didn't have one. I started to go in back of the house, but Marina called to me and said the neighbors would see me and I should walk down by the river.

WHEN I RETURNED HOME I had a bonanza of mail. Two *Newsweeks*, a book on quilting, six letters, and a stack of mystery books by E. B. James who writes about Seattle.

Chusita's youngest daughter was being married in the capital that weekend. I was invited to the wedding but felt I shouldn't take the time off as I would be gone for the next two weeks. Moses, Chusita's husband, and most of her family were staying at the house. I was surprised to see a television set in the dining room and that her family had brought videos. If there was any television watching, it was in the privacy of the bedroom. I'd not been aware of it ever being used.

My second son Clark, his friend Mary, and my fourth son Jim had toured and bird watched in Costa Rica for a week. I met them at the airport, and we planned to spend the better part of the week in Guatemala and then fly to Equador and on to the Galápagos Islands. Clark brought mail and Christmas presents, as well as books. I had decided I was reading too much junk and had him bring Tolstoy's *War and Peace*, which I had tried unsuccessfully to read before, *Don Quixote* and *Paradise Lost*.

Everyone in Llano Grande was curious to see my sons. Jim became Jamie, the J pronounced as an H; Mary, Maria; and Clark remained Clark. We toured the puesto, Linda looking very pregnant, little "Margarita" being due the first of March. We walked to two aldeas and watched some men cutting adobe bricks, admired the oven where Marina had just baked a sweetbread, and chatted with people we met.

I fixed stir-fried chicken with vegetables and cashew nuts served over rice, homemade brown raisin bread, peanut butter cookies and fresh pineapple and cantaloupe.

We took the long bus ride to Guate, stowed most of our belongings at the Villa Española Hotel, and bussed to Lake Atitlán. Panajachel on the lake was touristy, but has good shopping. The boys and Mary found woven bags reinforced with leather, and I bought several woven table runners with a poinsettia design to send back for gifts. We had a night in the capital before we left for Equador. I tied up loose ends while the rest of the family explored the underground market downtown.

Our TRIP TO EQUADOR via Panama happened the night before the United States military invasion there. We had been joined by a Cuban woman who was a U.S. citizen visiting a Peace Corps friend in Guatemala. Going through customs at the airport, Clark's, Jim's and the Cuban woman's passports were taken from them, along with seven other passengers' passports. It was the longest night I had ever spent. Our plane didn't leave until 2:00 A.M. Mary and I worried about Jim and Clark, and we knew nothing about the U.S. intervention. Jim had several cameras around his neck and wondered if the authorities suspected he was a reporter. The thought crossed his mind it was possible he might be jailed and beaten.

After an interminable six hours, we were conducted toward the exit, the passports returned, and we were escorted by soldiers to the plane. After arriving in Guayaquil at 6:00 A.M., we had a six-and-a-half-hour wait for the plane to the islands.

THE GALÁPAGOS, explored by Charles Darwin in the 1800s, lie three hundred miles from the mainland and had been declared a national park. The entry fee for each of us was fifty American dollars.

We were not disappointed. The beaches were like white sugar, and as in Darwin's time, birds are unafraid of humans and baby sea lions waddle up to be petted. We met a German couple looking for eight other people to fill a charter boat. Tourists are allowed only on boats and accompanied by a naturalist.

There was a young Australian couple working their way around the world, three Germans and an Englishman, all of whom were decent and congenial. Hans suggested we buy small gifts to exchange at Christmas and put in some money for a Yule punch bowl. The food was not particularly good and the ship had more than its share of cockroaches, but my year in Guatemala had made me less persnickety. I taught the crew how to make rice pudding, which Mary insisted was the only good food we had.

Christmas day found us snorkeling among diving penguins, seals and sea lions. We saw huge frigate birds displaying bright red pouches in their mating ritual and saw giant turtles whose tracks to the water were the size of treadmarks from a truck. The land and marine iguanas sunned themselves on the beaches, and we identified mockingbirds, nesting blue-footed boobies, finches, warblers and flamingos. Lovely tropic birds circled, trailing long white tail feathers.

Most spectacular were the great sea lions, in Spanish, *wolves of the sea*. The bulls were scarred from fighting to protect their harems. These huge animals lie in the sun all day at the edge of the water, swimming to cool off and fish.

While Clark and Mary chose to wait at the airport for our return flight, Jim and I took a taxi into Guayaquil. I bought gold hoop earrings for Linda and a T-shirt for Barbara for Christmas. As it was soon to be New Year's Eve, we were fascinated by the life-size effigies made of straw in the streets. Filled with firecrackers, when lighted, they symbolized doing away with the old and bringing in the new year.

We wondered how we would be routed home. The headlines and articles in local papers were hostile to the U.S. This time we stopped in El Salvador, which was having its own war, and then went on to Miami. It was strange being in the United States. We had lunch at the airport, and as it was my birthday, I had a rousing rendition of *Happy Birthday*.

My return to Guatemala was via El Salvador again, and I returned to my usual hotel where Barbara was waiting and wondering what had happened to me. She took me out to dinner for my birthday.

January 1990

When I returned to Llano Grande, I was told that Carolina was gone. Eloisa had mentioned that they had had her since she was a newborn. Apparently, her natural mother, who had been living up in the Petén in northern Guatemala, demanded the child, and Carolina had chosen to go with her. When I asked Eloisa if she contacted the police or a lawyer, she said they had no legal adoption papers for her and there was nothing they could do. I had always felt sorry for the child who seemed to do more than her share of the chores and was not allowed to attend 4-H meetings as did other girls her age. The birth mother was pregnant with a seventh child and I guessed felt Carolina at age ten could be some help to her.

I was concerned about Rosa, Petronia's daughter-in-law and Nixon's mother, and had asked Luis, a young man working for a private agency in family planning, to come up to talk to her. Luis said his degree was in agriculture but he had been working for the agency for over a year.

Climbing the hill to Carmen and picking our way over the rocky path to Rosa's house, we were greeted by eight yapping half-grown puppies who clearly disliked our intrusion. Rosa, about eight months pregnant, greeted us warmly and asked us to sit on her porch.

Luis kindly and patiently explained that her uterus, which he called matrix, was like soil and that you could grow good corn only when you had fertile earth. Since she had six living children, all of them malnourished and one with a deformed arm, this was enough. Everyone, both mother and baby, were healthier when the children were spaced.

I would have been willing to pay for a tubal ligation after that baby, but for that to happen, she needed the permission of her husband and to have had at least four living children. I didn't mention a vasectomy for her alcoholic husband might be a good idea. She listened politely and we walked to Petronia's house, as she was a midwife and we explained it all to her. On the way back the snarling, yappy puppies came running our way, and I thought family planification for them was justified as well!

THE SERMON THAT SUNDAY was unusual, being on how husbands and wives could be good to each other. Pablo used a flip chart and listed "relations sexual" as a second on the list. He was more progressive than I had given him credit for.

The next day I spent weighing and measuring children. On the whole the babies were clean, but I had bought some fabric printed with animals and had Marta make me an apron. It kept my blouses clean and the children could look at the colorful cats and dogs.

Because the bus broke down on the way, it took me nine and a half hours to get to Matequescuintla. I felt Leisl and I were prepared for our two-day classes. We had packets from Peace Corps for each teacher, with posters and cartoons and drawings useful in teaching health and nutrition. As Guatemalans love certificates, we bought diplomas and crayons and tape. We boiled eggs for sandwiches and bought juice. Leisl stayed up until 2:00 A.M. coloring posters.

We were up by 5:30 to make egg salad sandwiches and wash and slice cantaloupe when Liz came over to help us carry everything to the community center.

There were ten teachers and we played "Simon Says" as an introduction to naming body parts. I talked on the importance of teaching health in school. Liesl showed a drawing of an emaciated boy, and we discussed why Juan could be so malnourished. I bought a baby chick, which I concealed in a box. We discussed whether it could be—alive? did it breath? could it see?—all the time loud peeps coming from inside the box. We had the teachers pair up and asked each team to do a presentation the next day.

That night we spent up the mountain at Liesl's house. At dusk we sat on her porch drinking screwdrivers made from Tang and watched the stars come out.

We were lucky the next morning to catch a ride with a young farmer driving a new truck. He said he planned to go to Los Angeles the next month, which would involve eight days on a bus, and then secure a "coyote" to take him across the desert. I asked him if he feared the police, and he said, "Yes."

The second day of class went smoothly. We handed out evaluation sheets, the only criticism being our Spanish could have been better. This was directed to me, as Liesl was fluent.

Barbara had gone home to Lafayette, but I stayed in her house where Liz and I dispatched two scorpions we saw lying flat on the kitchen wall. Barbara said later that she had never encountered one.

I left Mateque at 4:30 A.M. The bus was not crowded and I was comfortable in jeans, wool sweater, down vest, hat and scarf. I could see the Southern Cross in the morning sky. There were banks of white hydrangeas and calla lilies, and behind the gauze curtain of clouds were the silhouettes of long-needled pines and cypress.

BECAUSE THE GOVERNMENT had not paid the bill for oil, there was no diesel in the country for buses. I was due to meet Liesl in Jalapa before our presentation for the Llano Grande teachers. Luckily, Renaldo, the sixth grade teacher, drove me to town. I told him I had been given $100 for scholarships for his students to go to junior high and needed him to pick the recipients as I didn't know who needed help. He said that the amount would pay tuition for a year for five students.

I waited a long time at the dentist's office for Liesl. She finally came, saying she had ridden in the back of a truck under a tarp for three hours and caught one of the few buses to Jalapa. The dentist was just leaving, but agreed to see us the next day.

We walked the mile and a half to June and Barry's house, only to find them gone, but luckily Michelle came by on her bike and produced a key for us. We had bought groceries, fixed our dinner, and were both so tired we went to bed early.

A quick trip to the dentist gave us thirty pages to copy on the importance of fluoriding teeth. That accomplished, with Liesl carrying a heavy box of teaching materials, we looked for some way to get to my aldea. One taxi driver wanted the equivalent of five dollars and another twice as much. We were surprised to find a bus that would take us as far as the Llano Grande exit and then were lucky to get a ride in a truck carrying broccoli.

Paying that driver the equivalent of a dollar, we bought a huge bag of broccoli for fifty centavos or about ten cents.

The second workshop went better than the first, although we did the same things. Eight teachers came, plus Linda and five health promoters, and Alvaro, the agriculture representative.

The teachers colored materials in the health books we had brought, acted out one of the stories from *Mariquita Cochinita*, the little pig, and particularly enjoyed playing musical chairs. For music we used the tooth-brushing song I had written and taped. They liked the raw vegetables dip, made from mayonnaise and catsup, and the egg sandwiches, asking for the recipes!

We had just about given up on the dentist coming with his fluoride project and were ready to go home when a white jeep arrived carrying the dentist, the medical chief of the area, and another man. The dentist brought slides, which he projected showing how to use fluoride, but interspersed with pictures he had taken in Washington, D.C. They were totally unrelated to dental care, and we saw the Lincoln Memorial, the Washington Monument, and the White House, along with children rinsing, teachers mixing the fluoride solution, and lines of children waiting for their cup of rinse.

However, the upshot was that the teachers were comfortable in dispensing it weekly and seeing that it was used correctly. The fluoride was provided by UNICEF. Later, eight-months-pregnant Linda and I walked to several nearby schools where she talked to teachers. Five hundred children received fluoride that year.

It was time for Servet to leave, having completed his six months' public health internship. Linda and I had a party at the puesto and invited the health promoters. We served fruit salad and banana bread and I made some lemon coconut cookies. The entertainment was two games the girls suggested. One was *Pata Pata* (meaning duck duck). The person who was "It" tried to guess who it was. There were gales of laughter. The other game was played even more enthusiastically. "It" (being Servet) was blindfolded and enticed into sitting on a water-filled balloon. He was a good sport.

I LEFT MY VILLAGE for a week in Antigua, where our nutrition group and Liesl's attended an annual in-service meeting.

Sitting through an extremely boring lecture in Spanish on the theory of learning, I thought Sergio could have come up with something more interesting. The lecturer, though Guatemalan, had attended Tulane University, but whether it had been presented in Spanish or English was of no help to any of us.

The conference lasted four days, but the plus for me was that my longtime friends, the Rosens, were in the city studying Spanish, and I had dinner with them each night. The Rosens had served in the Peace Corps in Zaire, Africa, where they worked in the bush, Susan as a nurse practitioner setting up baby clinics. We had a lot to share.

The next three days of the meeting were a little better, Sergio listening to our input and Liesl and I telling about the fluoride project. Most helpful was a video Nori had brought from California on bio-intensive gardening. The terrain near Palo Alto is much like that of Llano Grande, and the beautiful vegetables they were able to raise by amending the soil and deep digging was remarkable.

After the conference I spent the night in the capital and the next morning met Barbara at the airport. She had come back from a two-week vacation and it felt like Christmas. She had had my Galápagos slides developed, mailed about ten letters and several packages, and brought me a bonanza of gifts—a big wall calendar, a bag of pralines, two filled chocolate bars, several "roach hotels," and some roach poison. It was a strange, but appreciated, assortment of presents.

By FEBRUARY SCHOOL had not yet begun, and I had a week to get organized, to work on charlas, and go to both Carmen and Rinconada to set up times for women's groups. After nearly a year, everyone knew me, and I felt in control and comfortable in what I was doing.

Going up the road to Carmen, I found where Santos Gonzales lived. She had been to the health center the week before with a nine-month-old baby she was nursing, who was in fairly good shape, unlike her two- and six-year-olds, both of whom were clearly malnourished. Santos was pregnant again. Her husband had died within the last few months. She had borne twelve children, eight of whom had lived. Many times I had walked by her house and noticed a number of dirty, ragged children playing in the yard. No one in the family seemed to go to school. I brought Santos a bag of Incaparina and talked to her about growing vegetables, promising her seeds if she could find someone to dig up the soil.

I was working on a talk for rules on child nutrition which stressed breastmilk, beans, protein, and fruits and vegetables, when the new doctor arrived. She was another doctora, a large woman and not particularly attractive. She came with her parents and her nine-month-old baby boy. Roxane would live in the house next door to the puesto, which happened to be vacant. Linda said Rozan's husband was an intern as well at another site and the baby would stay with the grandparents.

I WAS HOPING TO GET MARINA'S bakery going. We fired up the oven and mixed up a batch of French bread, shaping it into rolls. While they were rising we baked molasses cookies from a recipe I used at home. As I couldn't find molasses, I had bought a brick of raw sugar, which Marina cut with her machete, and boiled it with water until it resembled molasses.

I used the oven thermometer Clark had brought, and according to that the oven wasn't as hot as before, but the cookies got done. We put more wood on the fire and the rolls baked in eighteen minutes.

Figuring the cost of cookies, Marina would have to charge fifteen centavos per cookie for a profit. Bread and rolls would most likely be a better choice, as sugar, margarine and eggs needed for cake and cookies made them expensive.

During my lunch hour I baked a Betty Crocker cake mix for Alicia's birthday, frosting it with pink icing mix and placing it on a platter surrounded by pink flowers. That evening Chusita, Goody-Two-Shoes, and the minister's family all had cake and punch.

IT WAS A GOOD MORNING at school. In all four classes I told the children one of the stories about Mariquita and had them act it out. We sang a song to the tune of *The Battle Hymn of the Republic* about "*Each day I wash with water and soap, cut my long fingernails, etc.*" Putting up the world map, I showed the students where I lived in the United States. With so many Guatemalans working there, people were familiar with cities but not states. I showed them countries I had visited in Southeast Asia and told them about my son Jeff who had spent over two years bicycling from Circle Alaska to Tierra del Fuego a few years before.

Later I walked down to Terrones to talk with the teachers about my teaching there. There would be three classes, and they welcomed the idea.

Terrones appeared more fertile and affluent. I stood in the shade of a giant ceiba tree growing along a barbed wire fence skirting a dry cornfield. Beyond was the soft green of a field of new tobacco, a ribbon of road, and the irrigation canal fronting blue-green acres of broccoli. I could see fields dotted with orange and banana trees as well as tropical trees I didn't know. The valley was circled by rolling foothills sparsely forested with pines and in the distance old volcanos.

One day I called on three mothers whose children were below weight. All the homes were clean, and I had the feeling none were super poor. They all seemed genuinely glad I had come. We talked about feeding the children four or five small meals a day and putting a little sugar in their milk for more calories and adding oil to their black beans. I explained about the four rules of some protein every day such as egg, Incaparina, or meat, a fruit or vegetable or both and the importance of drinking milk rather than sweetened coffee.

On THE FIRST DAY of teaching at Terrones, Linda showed me a shortcut and the walk took only twenty minutes. The school was surrounded by shade trees with a nice vegetable garden on one side. All the children wore shoes and appeared well dressed. I was totally taken aback when the sixth graders stood as I entered the room.

That afternoon I tried to get my slide projector to work, as the inside bulb did not light. I looked inside the lens and magnified was a giant cockroach along with its droppings. Disgusting!

The weather was definitely warming up. The only blooms at the puesto were cerise bougainvillea trailing over the chainlink fence and a few lemon-colored hibiscus. Pomegranates seemed to fruit and flower all year—the flowers, flame bells, above globes of maturing fruit. The Spanish name is *granada*, also the name of one of the loveliest cities in Spain.

Linda and I spent the afternoon weighing and measuring babies. She charted their growth from the graph I had made, and we added more

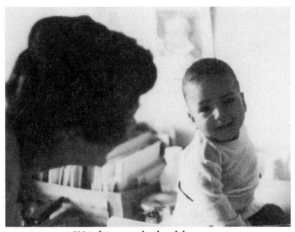
Weighing at the health center

names of malnourished children for me to visit. I asked her how little Margarita was and she answered with "*Muy contenta.*"

Chusita was having a well dug in hopes of a reliable water supply. It was dug entirely by hand and even her son Moses dug, although Arnoldo, the nephew, and a hired man did most of the work. Twenty-five meters down and still no water.

I talked to Chusita about the refrigerator needing defrosting, and she assured me it would be done the next day. I hoped so, or my chicken would spoil. I explained when there was a build-up of ice in the freezer that the door would spring as the other one had, and the refrigerator needed de-icing twice a month. Besides food, there was medicine and the popsicles she sold made from Kool-Aid. At times produce was stuffed on a shelf containing hiding cockroaches, and I didn't like to be surprised when I opened the door.

ON SUNDAY I ENJOYED SINGING in Spanish at church, although I needed a hymn book. Never having been involved with an Evangelical church, however, I couldn't get enthusiastic over songs with words and motions such as "*If you're happy in the Lord, clap your hands.*"

Suddenly, it turned cold. I was reading Cervante's *Don Quixote* in English, as I knew I'd never finish it in the original 17th Century Spanish. I wore my jogging suit to keep warm, which also served as "sleepers."

I BEGAN A NEW SCHOOL eight kilometers from Llano Grande at Piedra del Fuego, named for the flint found lying around.

No bus went up there, which meant a long walk. The children wore ragged clothing and were not as responsive as pupils at my other schools, perhaps because they didn't know me, but Freddy, the teacher who rode with the other teachers from Jalapa and then bicycled from Llano Grande, was delightful.

I had become so tired of playing lotteria with the Three Food Groups that I made another game with good health habits, such as fencing the chickens and keeping the cat off the table. In one of the squares I drew a picture of a fly swatter which was something new to the children.

I had brought my birding binoculars and was rewarded by seeing a gold-fronted woodpecker, called a *carpintaro*, a great kiskadee, and a giant wren.

That afternoon I was invited to four-year-old Otto's birthday party at the parsonage. Eloise had outdone herself with a three-dimensional rabbit cake. The whole Sunday School was invited, enjoyed a piñata, and we all had coffee with our cake, including the kids.

DUE TO LINDA'S PREGNANCY, she had a three months' maternity leave. At the health center I asked Irma how much she was paid a month and she said fifteen quetzales, around three dollars. Some days she worked eight hours.

I did a presentation on baby food up at Petronia's. There were always enough babies to sample what I had prepared, and with gusto they ate mashed bananas and cooked carrots. I read the mothers a sad story about a woman who had a baby who nearly died when he was fed cornstarch mixed with water instead of milk and acquired parasites from the unboiled water.

Marina and I baked bulgar wheat rolls in the new oven. I needed to get June back up there as the oven smoked. The rolls were delicious, light and fluffy and brown on the bottom. I used a couple of cups of bulgar I had soaked in water before adding it to a basic white bread recipe.

Back home there was still no water in the well even though they were down past twenty-five meters. Moses Jr. was on crutches and out of commission from having kicked a ball playing soccer, but he hadn't been doing much anyway. He looked so anorexic I asked Linda if she thought he could have AIDS. She thought most likely he used drugs.

ONE WEEKEND BARBARA and I met in Jalapa to meet two new volunteers, Trina and Gary. Trina was a nurse who had served in the Peace Corps in Africa while Gary was completing a master's degree in agriculture.

Barbara and I brought food over to June and Barry's house and fixed guacamole on fried tortillas, a chicken casserole of vegetables and spaghetti, cream and Parmesan cheese. They had just run out of gas, which was unavailable anywhere, but solved the problem by pulling out a two-piece ceramic stove they had made that used charcoal. I concocted a pie from cookie crumbs, instant pudding and green mango sauce.

On Sunday, I shopped for food for Linda's baby shower and in the afternoon baked two loaves of orange pecan bread and cooked a boiled dressing for the fruit salad.

All morning I worked at the puesto, and when I went home cut up a papaya (in Central America they are the size of a football), two cantaloupes, a pineapple and some bananas. When I returned, Linda had set up a big table laid with a plastic cloth and paper napkins. We placed a bunch of lavender and white baby's breath on the table and Maria from 4-H contributed plastic bowls and plates.

We had already begun to eat when the last guests arrived an hour and fifteen minutes late. Everyone clapped after Linda opened each present, and she received gifts such as safety pins, socks, and shirts. Barbara had sent a cotton sacque with "Baby" cross-stitched on the front, and I gave her diapers, a printed shirt, Q-tips and baby lotion.

IT WAS TIME TO BEGIN our mid-service physicals. Barbara and I met in Guate, and following instructions, left stool samples at a lab to be checked for parasites and amoebas. We both had appointments for physicals on Monday. The Rosens met us at our hotel, and we spent a pleasant afternoon at the textile museum. Nearby we found a Swiss pastry shop where we had lunch and extravagant desserts.

The Rosens had heard about a resort at a town called Amatitlán, an hour south of Guatemala City. We arrived by bus and checked into a nice hotel located on a lake and surrounded by gardens. There were three swimming pools which we used since the lake was polluted and covered with green algae.

We left the next day, taking a detour to a town called La Democracia. It had a large central park in which were a number of enormous carved heads of stone, thought to have been done by the Olmecs, who could have intermarried with the Toltecs, the origin of the Mayans. Later, I heard two theories of the heads—one that they were fertility symbols and the other the depiction of gods.

I HAD A PARTICULARLY FRUSTRATING time claiming a package at the customs office. A friend had sent me a CARE package with items such as toothpaste, toothbrushes, socks and a small bar of soap, and customs demanded over 100% of its value. I considered not accepting it as there was nothing I couldn't buy in Guatemala, but in case they sent it back, which was doubtful, I didn't want to hurt my friend's feelings. It took a week's salary for the fee. Later I told Liesl and she said she always cried at customs and had never had to pay for a package!

THE PEACE CORPS doctor told me I was very healthy, and Kathy, the nurse, made appointments for me to see a gynecologist and rheumatologist, and to have a mammogram. Later, everything was fine at the GYN's. The arthritis man said the pain in my hip was from bursitis and treatable and sent me off for x-rays, but Barbara got a call from Kathy that she was to report back to the mammogram center. I went with her and she was in the office a long time. The doctor found a large mass in one breast which would require a biopsy under anesthesia, for which she would be sent to Washington, D.C. We were sure Peace Corps did not expect her back as she had to make out reports of her work and have all her belongings packed.

I had a week of Spanish from a young teacher who neither enunciated clearly nor spoke slowly, but I appreciated the opportunity for further study.

March 1990

While I was gone, Linda's baby arrived. Goslier Huberto Gomez Veliz was a beautiful eight-pound boy who looked like his cousin, Carlito. Linda told me she had taken the bumpy bus by herself to Jalapa, done some shopping, and checked into the birthing center. Her labor was only an hour. I knew she was disappointed it wasn't "Margarita," but Goslier was strong and healthy.

SHORTLY AFTERWARDS, I was sitting in my room working on my quilt when a pretty young woman I had not seen before came in and invited Alicia and me to dinner for her birthday. She introduced herself as Liliana and she lived a block away near the school. When we arrived, I found her sister-in-law was a girl I knew named Argentina.

The house had a lovely patio surrounded by plants and ferns. Liliana served us soup with rice, a fruit drink I most likely should not have drunk (because of the possibility of unboiled water), chicken in sauce, and rice cooked with tomatoes and onions. Dessert was sugar cane, boiled and whipped. I had no idea why Liliana had singled out Alicia and me, and we chatted a while after dinner and played with our hostess's four-month-old baby girl.

Back home, another of Chusita's brothers had come to dig on the well. Hector was Arnoldo's father, who looked like and was as unfriendly as Cristobal, but a hard worker. Up to that time the well had cost forty-five hundred quetzales and still no water.

141

I WAS KNITTING ON A SWEATER for Goslier, while listening to Voice of America, when Liliana suddenly burst into my room with her baby and began to cry. She said both her mother-in-law and the baby's father hated her. She had been in Llano Grande since September and was miserable. She was nineteen and had lived with her grandmother after her parents left for the United States when she was thirteen and she had never heard from them again. Her in-laws told her she belonged in a mental hospital and she sobbed, "My baby is my life."

Chusita talked with her for a while and said she could spend the night. I kept the baby while the two of them went for her belongings. Later, Chusita said Liliana was really unbalanced and the baby's father's family were good people. She and the baby shared Chusita's bed, keeping her awake most of the night. Liliana stayed the next day and then left for her grandmother's house. I wondered what would happen to her and the baby, but never found out.

I RECEIVED A NOTICE from Peace Corps that we had gotten a raise in salary, the only problem being that with inflation we received forty dollars less than before. The quetzal was then five to the dollar.

LITTLE GOSLIER WAS BOUND from below the knee and across his thighs like a little Indian—Linda said for three months. She didn't explain why. I was surprised to see he was wearing a red bead fastened to his little wrist, the Mayan sign warding off the *ojo*, evil eye.

CHUSITA WAS LEAVING for Guatemala for gall bladder surgery. In addition, there would be no mail for over a month; however, I could go to the post office in Monjas to pick mine up whenever I wanted to.

I HAD A STRANGE EXPERIENCE both going up to Carmen and coming back. To give Linda some rest and for company, I

142

took Carlito with me. A young boy joined us whom I hadn't seen before. He told me he was fourteen. Carlito was tired and we sat down on the side of the road to rest under a pine tree. The strange boy cuddled up to me, took my hand and told me what soft hands I had, and the next thing I knew his hand was on my thigh. I left immediately, gave him my basket to carry, clutched Carlito and hurried to Petronia's house. I talked about vitamin A, passed out carrot sticks, which none of them had ever eaten raw, and gave them carrot seeds to plant.

I wasn't happy to find the strange kid waiting as we started down the hill. He tried to put an arm around my waist but was so short he wasn't able to reach that far. Telling me I was *gordita* (fat), a compliment in that culture, a light flashed that he was sexually aroused. Looking down, there was no question. I wanted to laugh, but needed to find the words for "get lost." Telling him I was old enough to be his grandmother and that I only held hands with little children, I snatched Carlito and we walked down the hill in record time. I couldn't wait to tell Linda and Alfonso about the amorous fourteen-year-old Don Juan!

THE MEN WERE DOING some blasting at the bottom of the well, but still no water. It was windy with a cloud cover which made the temperature bearable. The cicadas had begun their buzzing for the first time since last spring.

June came up to check on Marina's oven. She had had a bout with diarrhea, and whatever I had eaten or drunk at Liliana's house had caught up with me as well.

As the Guatemalan extension woman had predicted, June said none of the oven owners had gotten together and made a go of a successful bakery.

Marina had patched the inside of the oven. One problem was that the door did not fit correctly and there was considerable heat loss. We placed a metal comal in front of the fire box and started the fire. In the meantime, I mixed a batch of bread sticks, figuring they cost about a quetzal, and Marina would make a profit. It was clear none of her neighbors were willing to help her.

As June was explaining to Marina that she needed to know how much her ingredients cost to subtract that amount from the asking price, Marina's incredibly dirty two-year-old sneezed all over June's hands and the paper she was holding. On our way down the hill, June said, "Marge, I'm about ready to start a family, but after being around Marina's child, I'm not sure I can handle being a mother."

We gave half the bread to Marina and had some for lunch at my house with cheese, sliced tomatoes, milk and mango pie. June left on the afternoon bus, and I felt bad enough to take some Lomotil and go to bed. That night it was so hot I needed only a sheet over me.

I took a bus to Monjas in order to go to the post office and had four welcome letters. A friend had enclosed an article from the *Seattle Post-Intelligencer* on a quote of my son Jim. At that time he was working for an organic produce cooperative, and President Bush had been quoted as saying he did not eat broccoli. When a reporter asked Jim for a comment, he said, "Let him eat cake."

I felt incommunicado as the mail was not coming to Llano Grande and Alicia said she was not able to accept telegrams. That was the situation until Chusita returned from her surgery.

As of April 1, it had cooled off a little. The clouds were apricot colored, cicadas were buzzing and a gentle wind ruffled the banana leaves. Communion Sunday again with the grape Kool-Aid "wine."

April 1990

All was not well with Linda. She seemed agitated, unable to settle down or sit still. She moved all the furniture around at the puesto—I'm sure without Alfonso's help. He asked me if I thought she was behaving normally and I said, "No, she's been through a difficult time and needs love, patience and rest."

The next day Linda said she was having a party for all the children in town and I was to bring thirteen dozen oatmeal cookies. She asked me to go home for my camera, and when I returned she'd put on maternity clothes, stuffed a pillow in front, and wanted me to take some pictures.

Roxane was to have helped me with the cookies, but as usual was not around. I baked them in Maria's kitchen using her toaster oven. Why Linda would consider having a party for seventy-five when she had a two-week-old infant was ridiculous.

The following day Renaldo was giving tests, so I only taught the first and third graders. Later, I went to the puesto where two friends of Linda's were cutting out large pink hearts for wall decorations. The usually clean room was a mess, things scattered around, the floor dirty, and Carlito wore a huge sweat shirt he had slept in. Linda was feeding the baby sugar water from a bottle, as she decided he was colicky. I thought the poor child was most likely hungry as Linda seemed too agitated to calmly sit or lie down to nurse him. I had brought some booklets I'd found in Spanish on breast feeding.

Hurrying back to my house, I quickly made a sandwich and returned to the puesto. The big pink hearts on the wall said, "Goslier, First Party, April 3, 1990—Carlito."

Linda concocted a terrible tasting punch to which she had added iodine pills. She was wearing a dirty smock and the place was still in shambles
when people began to arrive. I took Carlito to the bedroom, washed him,
combed his hair and dressed him in white shorts, a clean T-shirt and knee
socks.

Outside in the yard a number of small children were playing. The mayor's
dog from across the street had come in the gate and was jumping at the
children. Without thinking, I took hold of his collar and put him out,
something I had always done with my own dogs, when he sunk his teeth
in my right hand at the base of my thumb. Besides bleeding profusely, it
was painful. Instructions in training, if bitten, were to wash the wound
with quantities of water and get to the capital immediately for more rabies
shots.

Dripping blood through the puesto, I washed my hand with surgical
soap, and Alvaro, from agriculture, poured panfuls of water on it.

Servet had borrowed his father's car and arrived with Roxane. He was
put to work decorating a piñata, and some of us tied yarn around tiny
plastic baby bottles to pin on our clothes. I made Linda sit down and
nurse Goslier. Servet said he would take me to Guate that evening.

Marta, the seamstress, came with a strange looking christening outfit
for Goslier. It was white with blue and yellow ribbons, an eyelet underskirt,
complete with a cap and mittens.

Meanwhile, Linda appeared again in her maternity clothes with a pillow in front. There was a crowd of people in the room and more outside
when suddenly Linda began a long, tearful, and impassioned speech about
her life and troubles with a lazy husband.

We were embarrassed and astonished when she went to the examining
room, climbed on the table, and instructed Servet to deliver her baby. "You
have an eight-pound baby boy," he said. I felt I needed to say something,
and added, "and he has all his clothes on." Fortunately, at that point Linda's
mother arrived. I found out later that Maria had sent her husband for her
in his truck. Carman burst into tears and took her daughter to her room to
comfort and change clothes. "Linda is having a post partem depression," I
said to Servet, and he agreed.

Linda, looking a little better, opened presents people had brought. I
was really not aware this was another baby shower she was giving for
herself until then. Carman took Linda and the baby to her home outside of

Jalapa, where hopefully she could get some rest, be able to calmly feed the child, and get her family's life back in order.

Servet and I didn't leave until after 6:00 for Guate. There was a considerable amount of construction on the road and the doctor drove at top speed. When he asked me if I was *nerviosa*, I told him, "Yes." Between his driving, Linda's obvious depression, and the fact that my hand was still bleeding, I was indeed nerviosa.

The hotel where Barbara and I always stayed had room for me and offered to call a doctor, but I told them I would see the Peace Corps nurse in the morning and be fine. The porter asked me about Barbara and if she were *gravis*. Gratefully, I soaked in a hot tub before going to bed.

Feeling a great deal better the next morning, I went to the Peace Corps office for my shot and was told I'd need another Saturday and they would make arrangements for me to have it at the hospital as the office would be closed.

I got permission to use the diplomatic pouch in order to receive eight hundred toothbrushes my American Association of University Women friends had collected for me to use when I presented a dental unit in the schools.

It was disappointing when I called my friends in the U.S. to find they wouldn't be visiting me the next month as planned. They had recently returned from Losotho where they had worked in agriculture for Peace Corps.

After lunch I was so tired I slept for a couple of hours. With the Bakers not coming, having lived with no water for a week, the toilet out of order, no mail, Linda's breakdown, Barbara's problems, and to top it off, I discovered my Visa card had expired, everything seemed to have gone wrong.

Kathy, the nurse, had given me a toll free number in Washington where I could call Barbara. She reported the doctor could find nothing amiss in the biopsy and they were sending her home to heal for two weeks. She would return for another mammogram and should be back in Guatemala the last of April. The porter gave me a big smile when I reported that Barbara was no longer *gravis*.

In the hotel lobby I met a Canadian woman who was trying to call her embassy to find a doctor. She had left a tour group because she had become ill and was alone. We left by taxi for the hospital Peace Corps used and she was treated for an ear infection, bronchitis and tourista. She felt well enough to have a sandwich with me at the Swiss deli and we picked up several prescriptions for her at a pharmacy.

The following day I took her to the textile museum which displays the lovely weaving, embroidery and costumes done by the Mayans. I told her about my work and the dental song I had written. She said her daughter-in-law had visited Cuba and come home with a tooth song the children sang in school there and promised to send it to me.

After getting my second rabies shot, I left Guate for home. In Jalapa I ran into Laura, Linda's sister, who reported Linda was on medication, had slept ever since she had come home and seemed better. I said I would come to their house after Easter.

At home I cleaned my dirty room, finding a dead mouse on one shelf and cockroaches again in my files. The toilet was barely usable but better than the family latrine. I was surprised they used newspaper in place of toilet paper, as it was sold in the pharmacy, but apparently old habits are hard to break.

Alfonso came over and said Linda was both eating and sleeping. She was fortunate to have a capable and sensible mother.

It was overcast with a slight breeze, which was a nice change from the heat that made it difficult to sleep. There must have been a new hatching of little black ants as they were everywhere. The only thing to do was not to have anything around they could feed on. I baited again for both roaches and mice.

LOUISE, A VOLUNTEER WORKING in the small animal program an hour away, invited me to spend the weekend. She was in her fifties, had had a series of unhappy marriages, and a miserable time in the Peace Corps. She loved animals more than people and was appalled by the cruelty shown to them in Guatemala. Opinionated, and not popular with volunteers, she was, however, kind and sensitive to anything with four legs.

Louisa's cat had caught a mouse and instead of eating it, kept it for a playmate. She carried it around in her mouth, depositing it in one of Louisa's shoes to sleep. The mouse was fed cat food soaked in milk, his "mouse dish" being a bottle cap. Everyday the cat and mouse played together, and when the mouse had had enough, it retreated to a spot behind a shovel which stood against the wall. All this was charming until much to Louisa's horror she found the mouse smothered as the result of the cat napping on top of the "mouse bed" shoe. Louise was devastated by the mishap and cried for a long time.

I LEFT THE NEXT DAY for the capital for doctor's and dentist's appointments. The bus driver, Louise had mentioned, was a former airline pilot. In excellent English he asked me if I were comfortable and told me to fasten my seatbelt. Asking where the stewardess was, he replied that she would be joining us at the crossing. Fifty miles toward Guate was a town called Barbarina where always an unattractive very fat woman boarded the bus to sell tortillas with sauce from a large basket. The woman made her rounds, and as she left the driver turned to me and said, "There was the stewardess."

The orthopedic doctor felt I didn't need any more cortisone, and the dentist repaired the tooth last year's dentist had filled and declared my root canal was in good shape. I ran into Liesl at the Peace Corps office, and we bought food at a supermarket across the street and shared a picnic lunch.

On the way home, after shopping in Jalapa, I got off in Monjas to pick up my mail. There was nothing for me, but I brought back some letters and telegrams to Llano Grande. Stopping at Linda and Alfonso's tienda, he reported that she was better and could be back in another week. I had hoped she would stay longer with her mother.

SCHOOL THE NEXT DAY did not go well. I had both the fifth and sixth graders take notes in their new notebooks on parasites and make drawings of different kinds of worms. That went well enough, but the sixth graders became totally out of control playing lotteria with health cards. I gave out stickers to the kids who had finished their drawings and there was a stampede. They were so tightly controlled that the students were unable to handle anything different or fun.

That afternoon I baked English muffins in my frying pan and they turned out beautifully. They would work as well on a comal, the tortilla skillet, and do well for a food demonstration for 4-H and my women's groups.

Roxane was still away, but I saw a friend of Linda's who said Linda was not much better. Maria said the baby was on a bottle, and that evening at dinner Alicia mentioned she had just seen Linda and her mother and the baby at the puesto. I ran over and thought Linda seemed relaxed, but Goslier seemed different, more like a little old man. Encouraging her to stay with her mother for a while, I told her I could come there on Saturday.

I always enjoyed Rosemary up at Rinconada. On the way back I made a date with Marina to bake the next week and she asked how much flour she should buy. When I suggested twenty-five pounds, she said she hadn't enough money.

Farther down toward town, I stopped at Milvea's house to talk to her about food for her year-old fussy eater. I had a special interest in the little girl as she was born at Chusita's shortly after I came. I suggested trying tiny tortillas made from black beans and cornmeal she could pick up herself, a drink of Incaparina, banana, Incaparina pancakes, and soup made from eggs and chipilin, the nutritious legume that grew wild. I hoped she wasn't given sweet rolls and sugared coffee.

I ARRIVED IN JALAPA and took a taxi to Linda's parents' house. Goslier was drinking from a propped bottle and Linda was fixing lunch in the kitchen. I had brought oatmeal chocolate chip cookies, and she sent home a jar of chicken and rice for Alfonso's dinner. I told her I would be catching the late bus and it was a long time for chicken to be unrefrigerated, but it didn't seem to bother her. Later, I told Alfonso to boil it well before he ate it.

School at Terrones was always a pleasure as the children were so polite. I returned home by way of the irrigation canal where fields of lush tobacco plants were a sea of pink spiked flowers. Alongside was stubble from a milpa and the remains of harvested broccoli. The new tomato plants had fruit the size of small green plums.

Back home the evangelical talk show blared loudly, but I managed to type some letters and recipes.

Roxane finally came back. All the young women in training to be health promoters opted to attend sewing classes at Maria's instead of coming to the puesto. I tried to pin the doctora down to a schedule where we could work together teaching health, but got nowhere. She did say that Alfonso had taken Linda to see a doctor in the capital. I was glad he was at least taking some responsibility. As there were few patients at the puesto, I had no babies to weigh and no one to do presentations for, so I spent my time translating *The Care of a Sick Child*.

That day it was so hot and humid I felt sticky just sitting still, but by night time rain was falling on the tile roof, making it cooler.

Having told Marina I would be up at Rinconada to bake English muffins, I was surprised to find her daughter, Juliet, babysitting as her mother had left for Jalapa that morning. Returning, I sat for a while on a rock by the river that divided dry rocky Llano Grande with its cactus, eucalyptus and parched grasses from verdant Rinconada where grew butter-yellow bamboo, pines and succulents.

Again it was rutting season, and Dobie came home with bleeding gashes on his ears and the top of his head split open to the bone. He whimpered most of the night.

As planned, I arrived at Barbara's house in Mateque, but found she had not returned. Elizabeth and I fixed tuna fish and noodles, carrot sticks and chard, and had M&M's for dessert. My first thought was to leave in the morning, but I had brought work to do and it was cooler there in the mountains. The next afternoon while I was lying in her hammock reading *Don Quixote* she returned. She had sent me a telegram asking me to meet her in Jalapa, but with the sometimes non-existent mail system, I had not received it. While we caught up on news, we had pork chops, noodles and fresh pineapple and then played gin rummy.

Elizabeth had been dating a young Guatemalan for some time and was puzzled that he had never asked her to visit his home or family. She was very upset when her Spanish teacher suggested he undoubtedly had other women. Roberto insisted there was absolutely no one else and was using the familiar "tu" form used for loved ones and children.

CHUSITA WAS BACK following her surgery. Now we could receive telegrams and mail. There was another unexplained holiday, meaning both schools and the health center were closed. I found candied fruit, cardamom, and raisins at the market and baked a Norwegian Christmas bread in my improvised oven.

At school we began a unit on care of the teeth. Seeing all the gold in the mouths of those who could afford it and the gaps or total toothlessness in those who could not, I was surprised the students' teeth were in fairly good shape. I had each child open his mouth and his seat-mate count cavities. For the next month we would concentrate on dental hygiene.

Later, Carlito and I climbed up to Carmen where I fixed carrot raisin salad, talked about parasites and played the new loteria of good health habits. That night my reading Cervantes was interrupted by high winds and thunder that knocked out the power.

A MEETING WITH MY new women's group at Elenora's was rewarding. She and her daughter, Tina, had asked me to meet with them and invited twenty women. I brought a calendar with pictures of Washington State, a map of the U.S. to show where I lived, and gave them samples of knitting and embroidery. After I discussed nutrition, we played the inevitable loteria.

The food demonstration was tortillitas made of Protemas, a soy meat substitute which I soaked in hot milk, and consommé, adding eggs, flour, grated carrots, potatoes and onions which resembled vegetable pancakes that we fried in hot fat. I hoped to have a good group going, which proved to be the case.

On Saturday I banked in Jalapa, took my clothes to the laundromat, and waited at Michelle's house until my bus left. She was in love with an El Salvadorian soccer player and they planned to marry. We had strict orders because of the political situation not to cross the border, but he would meet her bus and drive her by car to his city. I was surprised he was not better looking. He said his game in Guatemala was cancelled because terrorists had bombed the light plant and they needed to conserve power.

Eloisa told us that Maria Angelica's fourteen-year-old brother had been murdered by drunk *campesinos* (farm workers) over the weekend. It was strictly being at the wrong place at the wrong time around guns and alcohol. Olga, the mother, had an alcoholic husband, a dead son, whom Chusita claimed was a good kid, a younger son who had frequent epilepsy attacks, a six-year-old girl and the terribly malnourished two-year-old.

To beat the heat, I started for the school at Piedra del Fuego at 7:30 in the morning. It took me an hour and ten minutes to walk there, but I got a good look at a lovely yellow-backed oriole who popped out of her nest which resembled an unraveling knee sock. Her feathers of deep gold and black glistened in the sunlight. In addition, I saw a hummingbird, a yellow warbler and a woodpecker.

Drenched in perspiration, I walked down to Terrones to find the women preparing a vegetable salad for Mother's Day, obviously not expecting a meeting.

Back home I cleaned my bike, as I had decided to send it back with Sergio the following day. My rationale was that most of the roads were so bad that if I fell and broke an arm, hip or leg, it would be the end of Peace Corps for me. In addition, I was constantly being pestered by men and boys who wanted to borrow it.

THE SESSION WITH SERGIO went well. I was holding Gosher when he came to the puesto. He volunteered to go up to Olga's house with me to have a look at Maria Angelica. Sergio said she definitely had marasmus, calorie deficiency, but got nowhere talking to the mother about having the child hospitalized. Obviously she was grieving over the death of her oldest boy. Sergio had no answers about what we could do and said the next thing to happen would be her abdomen would swell. I had brought up a large can of whole powdered milk.

I fed Sergio cold gazpacho, homemade oatmeal raisin bread spread with egg salad, a jellied vegetable salad and iced tea. While we were eating lunch, I noticed at least one hundred cockroach casings on one wall of the dining room. The good news was that Sergio felt I was doing a good job!

I WAS INVITED TO A GOING AWAY party for Johanna, the plump blond who had so impressed our bus helper. She worked in Mateque, and I waited two and a half hours at a town toward Guate for a bus. I was joined by Louise who had been in her training group. The party was held at the home of two bachelors, friends of Johanna. There were about thirty people including volunteers, local townspeople and the mayor.

One of the women who had been in her training group was a delightful, funny woman named Roduska, age about fifty, a vocabulary like a longshoreman, and a bra size well over forty-five. As she bobbed up and down like a yo-yo while dancing with the mayor, he exclaimed, "This is just like dancing with Dolly Parton!"

I finally met Elizabeth's Roberto, who was incredibly handsome, but they must have had a tiff as they neither danced together nor acknowledged each other.

I spent the following day up at the mountain at Liesl's house, which was nestled on a little knoll with deep valleys on three sides. The surrounding hills were planted in coffee shaded by rows of banana trees. Dotting the landscape were a few pastel tile-roofed farm houses amongst pines, eucalyptus and juniper, and in the valley were splashes of fuchsia-colored bougainvillea. Just below me were single pink hibiscus with maroon stamens where several tiny hummingbirds gathered nectar. One word in Spanish for hummers is *picaflors*.

Liesl had translated a children's book we had begun together and I finished, which we called *Pepe and Patricia and Their Garden*. It told about a pair of twins who were given some money by their grandfather for their birthday, and instead of buying candy and soda, he talked them into seeds which he said were like magic and would last a long time. The nice woman at the tienda gave them each a popsicle and they happily went home. Following their grandfather's instructions, they planted, watered, and tended their garden. Later Grandma was able to make a delicious soup from the vegetables with carrots that looked like small suns, radish tops, and beans, that Pepe declared was the best soup he had ever eaten. Grandma remarked that gardens were like children, both needing care and love and sunshine. One of the teachers at Liesl's school went over the Spanish, and Stephanie had offered to illustrate the text. We felt good about our efforts.

Sometimes I felt as though I were a missionary, and often passengers on busses asked me why I was there. However, my message was "to encourage people to eat from the three food groups, have children inoculated, and be reasonably clean."

One day I had gone to a home to talk to the mother of two malnourished boys and was showing her examples of junk foods and empty calories. Pablo, the minister, came in wearing his huge Jesus Saves belt. He had come to talk with the boys' father, and I decided we each had our own goals and objectives.

FRANCESCA WAS A WIDOW about my age who lived a block from me and was one of the four "Avon" ladies. I ordered some face cream from her from a Spanish catalog and we talked about building an oven in her yard for starting a bakery. She was enthusiastic and I said I would look into the financing.

There was a new young man in town from an agricultural college sent to work with students planting school gardens. Both Alvaro and I were delighted, and I offered to supply seeds from the Peace Corps. Aida, the principal, was pleased, though Renaldo, the sixth grade teacher, was not enthusiastic. In addition, when I told him we would be practicing toothbrushing for my dental unit, he flatly said there was not enough water, but I decided we would do it anyway.

At the puesto I held the first baby we had seen with a confirmed case of kwashiorkor, a protein deficiency. He was fifteen months old and weighed as many pounds. Typically, he had edema, or swelling, long eyelashes and an orange cast to his hair. He had been hospitalized and had acquired a bad case of impetigo. The mom was pregnant again and I gave her a box of whole milk.

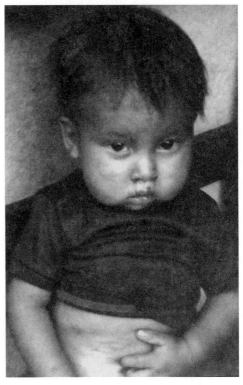

Protein deficiency (kwashiorkor)

THERE WERE DESERTED STRETCHES on the way to school at Piedro del Fuego. Just outside of Llano Grande I was joined by two men who were so drunk they had trouble walking. One of them was Maria Angelica's father and he asked me for help, which meant money. I told him I was there to teach and didn't have money and he should see the puesto doctor about getting help for his daughter. He finally left when I said I wanted to walk by myself.

Freddy, the teacher, was cooperative and helpful. He seemed to have a good rapport with his students, without intimidation or sarcasm. On the way home I identified a large blue bird with a long tail as a mot mot. Like the oriole, he was in the same spot each time I walked by.

AT THE END OF MAY it rained hard most of the night. Coming from the Pacific Northwest, I never realized how much I had missed it. Here it cooled things off, small plots of grass were beginning to sprout, and I found places where wild zinnias grew.

Don, the volunteer who took me shopping my first weekend at my site, was to be married to a beautiful Guatemalan teacher he had met at church. He was in the same small animal program as Louise, Roduska, and Johana, and in the same training group as June and Barry.

Early the morning of the wedding, I met Barbara for breakfast and shopping. I had made arrangements for a permanent on the top and sides of my hair, the results of which made me look much like a large poodle.

The wedding was held at the Evangelical church where I had done the nutrition program in November. The affair was supposed to have begun at 4:00, but we waited nearly an hour for the ceremony to begin. Don's mother from Pennsylvania and the mother of the bride led the procession, to the accompaniment of the march from *Aida*. They carried lighted candles and were followed by twelve bridesmaids wearing short pale blue dresses and carrying bouquets of artificial carnations. The bride was exquisite in white satin and a long train with a veil over her face.

The congregation consisted of at least two hundred Guatemaltecans, one hundred squirmy small children, and about twenty volunteers. After a long service including Bible readings, a sermon and hymns, Don kissed his bride and to the tune of the traditional wedding march led the way to the reception in the courtyard where we were served turkey tamales, coffee, and bread. One of the volunteers had made the wedding cake.

The following morning a number of us had breakfast with Don's mother, aunt and cousin, who were glad to talk with us, not being able to communicate

156

with the bride or her family. Tearfully, the mother added she couldn't even talk to her new daughter-in-law.

WE HAD HEARD ABOUT A SWIMMING POOL near Monjas, and Barbara and I discovered a natural pool set in a grove of mangoes fed by springs. There was even a picnic area with slides and swings for children. We were the only swimmers until we were ready to leave and a young man came shepherding a group of children over to talk. He said he was the nurse at a nearby normal school and each Sunday brought the students to swim. When I told him I was from Llano Grande, he said he was Alicia's brother.

ONE MORNING I WAS ALONE at the health center and heard a knock on the door, only to find a tall blond gringo. Assuming he was a volunteer, I asked him in and he said he and his wife were missionaries in a town twenty-five miles away and were adopting Santo's granddaughter. He needed a form filled out by the midwife who had delivered the child in order to secure a legal adoption. Santos, who was expecting a child of her own, was openly hostile and appeared angry, even though the baby's mother was sixteen (this was her second child), unmarried, and unable to care for her. It did not occur to the grandmother that the child would grow up in a privileged home and most likely be college educated. I knew who the midwife was, showed him her house, and invited him to lunch when he had finished.

The following day, when I had returned from school and arrived at the puesto, Paulina, the emaciated little woman with the four children whose house Linda and I had visited a few months before, was waiting on the porch with a friend. Inside, she lifted her skirts to show me the blood-soaked towel between her legs. I quickly ran next door to tell Roxane, who was eating lunch, that she was needed immediately. The doctora was clearly annoyed, saying she did not care to be bothered and to tell the patient to return later. I said this was an emergency and the woman might not be alive later. Reluctantly, Roxane walked to the puesto, and sizing up the situation asked Pauline if she were pregnant, to which she replied, "No, I have no husband." The patient, in pain, slumped onto a chair and fainted.

Roxane and the friend lifted her to the examining table and the doctor started an I.V. She sent me to the farmacia for a new bottle of glucose, and when I returned Paulina opened her eyes and asked who would pay for it. I told her not to worry.

It was decided I should accompany Paulina to the hospital in Jalapa. The first plan was that Alfonso would drive us to the highway in his new truck and we would wait in the sun for a bus. I told them Paulina could not do that. Next, a truck appeared with Daniel, the agriculture student, who drove us to Jalapa, while I held Paulina, praying she would not hemorrhage to death in the hour it took to get there.

I was with the patient in the emergency room while the doctor examined her and his diagnosis was "abortion." Later, when I asked Linda how Paulina had done it, she said most likely taken herbs women knew were effective. Neither abortion nor hemorrhage were words I was particularly anxious to add to my Spanish vocabulary.

It came out that Linda was seeing a psychiatrist in the capital. Maria said Linda was far from well and still very angry, and Alicia added that Linda thought she was well but was not.

We still had no mail delivery. I made a special trip to Monjas and found Linda and Alfonso had picked it up. I was disappointed to find my only mail for a week was a padded envelope containing three paperbacks and went to bed depressed. The next afternoon I was pleasantly surprised to find the rest of my mail on my table, a pile of recipes, a note from a former college roommate, and a long letter that had been with the books. Strangely, they were without envelopes.

It TOOK THREE BUSES for Barbara and me to get to Puerto Barrios for another bird count. The main hotel was full and another, a block away, could only be described as a pit.

We were assembled before 5:00 and walked a trail above the beach, and in all identified forty-five species. By 1:00 in the afternoon we decided we were ready to swim in the ocean. Standing on the beach afterwards, we acquired at least a thousand "no seeum" bites.

That night the group had a late dinner, and I tried the local dish which was a soup made with coconut, cooking bananas, crab, sea snails, shrimp and fish. I thought I wouldn't order it again, as I didn't care for cooked bananas. We decided to catch the bus that left at 1:30 A.M. and picked up our tickets, which was a good choice as our room was over 100°, crawling with cockroaches, had no water, and the noise from the disco next door made sleep impossible. Until the bus left, we were drenched with perspiration, but as soon as we began to move, we were both able to sleep until 5:30 when we got off on the highway to wait for the Jalapa bus.

LINDA HAD BEEN HOSPITALIZED in Guatemala City. Since the nutritionists and nurses had been invited to a Pan American nutrition conference, I was anxious to attend and could visit Linda as well. I registered at the Dorado Hotel where the conference was held and was able to walk to the hospital. I bought a bunch of red roses from a stand on the street and explained to the social worker at the hospital who I was. She had a nurse check on Linda and reported she was worse, and too *triste* (sad) for visitors. She did take the flowers to her.

There were several hundred delegates from Central and South America, beautifully dressed and groomed. The only bare legs were those of volunteers. Besides some Peace Corps members from Honduras, the affair was attended by educators, doctors and researchers. It was the first time I had met upper-class, educated, Latin Americans.

The first day was technical: nutrition and sports, nutrition internal, research on the state of vitamin A on the population of a small town in Guatemala, and the metabolism of vitamin A. The latter would have been hard enough to understand in English.

In the lobby food distributors provided samples of soup, crackers, cheeses, juice and granola bars. The next day there was an excellent session I could understand on oral health and nutrition. We were all invited to a German Club I didn't know existed, set in a park amid swimming pools, lawns, flowers and tennis courts. In a tropical downpour, we were taken in vans for a lunch provided by a pasta company, consisting of pasta prepared ten ways, soft drinks and cookies.

I asked Cindy, the nurse from my nutrition group, to share my room with me. We had French onion soup and salad for dinner and took a bus to the national theater for a free performance of the folk ballet. Afterwards, we swam and then soaked in the hotel's hot tub.

There were several consumer programs from Peru, but the highlight was talks by candidates for president telling what they would do about nutrition if elected. One stated all mothers should nurse their babies, but Rios Mont, the terrible secretary of state during the worst of the killings, insisted the nutrition problem was spiritual!

Both Mario and Sergio attended some of the sessions, and Sergio said he had tried to visit Linda as well but had not been allowed to see her even though he was a doctor.

The last day, Kellogg's cereal put on a breakfast with fruit plates, different kinds of cereal, muffins, juice and coffee. Christine, from my training group, invited me to come home with her to a town an hour and a half away which was largely indigenous. The populace spoke Kachique and women wore lovely purple and gold blouses with their gathered skirts.

The surrounding area was green, wooded, and the farmers grew flowers for export. Christine had the biggest and nicest Peace Corps house I had seen, decorated with rugs and baskets. She had a gas stove with a real oven. The town was fairly near the hospital where I had taken Gloria, and some of her work was putting on nutrition workshops when parents came to visit their hospitalized children.

Returning home, I had a stack of mail. Alfonso had called the hospital and reported that Linda had improved and was being released. I cooked chicken and homemade noodles and baked a marble cake I shared with the family.

The school garden looked beautiful. Danielo had left, but unfortunately, there was no plan for weeding the plot.

Barbara and I met in Jalapa for an eight-hour bus trip to a town called Esquipulas, reached by unpaved roads through the mountains near Honduras. The city was a tourist destination, very clean with many hotels and pensións. In about 1758 a huge church was built that became a famous pilgrimage center. In January, crowds of people come to worship and pay penance—the main attraction being a black Christ carved of citrus wood by a famous sculptor. Many of the Mayan temples had been burned by the conquistadors, and in 1559 an Indian had a vision of a black Christ. As there were some black deities, Spanish priests thought this might make Catholicism more acceptable.

The church was set in a lovely park, and the Christo Negro was encased in glass behind the altar. We sat in the back listening to the organ and mass and, besides a boys' choir, there were at least a dozen priests.

In the background were still aqueducts that brought water to a fountain between the church and town center. We walked to a hotel on a hill and spent the day swimming and relaxing by the pool. We could have had dinner there but neither of us was particularly hungry.

GENERALLY, MONDAYS WERE BUSY for me, but that day there was no school, no 4-H and no doctora. Alfonso reported Linda could be home at the end of the week and back to work the week following.

After much badgering on my part, all the teachers finally nailed a strip of wood to the wall and pounded in the nails I had provided for hanging up each child's toothbrush. I made a poster with Margarita's "perfect twin" who also had perfect teeth. Underneath I lettered, "This or This? Your Choice." For the next month we practiced brushing and flossing each time I came, before the children took their toothbrushes home.

At my women's groups I baked English muffins on a comal. It worked out nicely as I could mix the yeast dough and while it rose give my talk on health and play some games. I cut the muffins out with an empty tuna can and they baked quickly.

At Terrones, Tina again mentioned they thought I should marry their Uncle Pedro. The time before he had sat leering at me while I talked about rehydration. Uncle Pedro was a campesino of undetermined age who wore a straw hat, had a straggly mustache, and sat scratching his stomach. I told them I wasn't very good at making tortillas, which

Women's group talk on rehydration

they thought was very funny. This time I said my Spanish wasn't good enough, which they found hilarious. The next time I would mention I wasn't Catholic!

I HAD BROUGHT BACK from the capital a video on bio-intensive gardening which Alvaro and I previewed to show at church. The video was in English and I translated for around thirty-five adults and sixty children.

That Sunday at church we were divided into groups, and I was assigned to the social service section. The church needed money for food, medicine and clothes and wondered how they could raise some money. I offered to get some appropriate films and invite the town and charge money, but Eloisa said they couldn't ask anyone to pay at church. I thought about a cookbook, but it would cost more to print than we could take in on sales. It occurred to me later that perhaps they expected me to give them money.

AT THE HEALTH CENTER I swept up bandages, dirt, broken glass and papers, took all the plants off the counter and watered them, and dusted, and then mopped the floor. It began to rain again, which meant the floor would be filthy as soon as patients came. That evening as I was working at the table in my room, Linda popped in with Carlito. Her face looked puffy, she had not lost any of her tummy, and I wondered if she were on some potent tranquilizer.

Stephanie arrived the next day. I had expected her the night before, but she had gotten to Jalapa too late to make the Llano Grande bus and had spent the night with June and Barry. She took a bus to the turnoff and walked the four kilometers to my house.

She reported she was disgusted with both the doctor and some of the nurses at the hospital where she worked. As she had said before, the doctor was drunk much of the time and one of the nurses picked all the vegetables for herself that she had expressly grown to feed the malnourished children under her care.

I particularly wanted her to see Maria Angelica, and since she was a registered dietitian, thought she might have some ideas about helping her.

162

At twenty-six months, the child was finally strong enough to stand by herself, but Stephanie didn't have any new ideas.

At breakfast we were talking about going to Jalapa, where Stephanie wanted to have her hair curled, when Chusita overheard us and said that Gilda, a pretty new health promoter, had a beauty shop in town; that was news to me. Gilda was glad for the business and all the neighborhood children peeked through the window to watch the gringa have her hair curled.

That night we baked a flan and Stephanie made a peanut saté sauce that we

Market in Jalapa

served over rice and stir-fried vegetables, which was truly gourmet!

July 1990

It was time for another Fourth of July celebration, and this time was held at the U.S. Marine's complex in a posh section of the capital. The mansion that housed the marines who guard our embassy was walled, enclosing a huge lawn with flower beds, a volley ball court and swimming pool.

In the kitchen were pots of chili, to which we added more tomato sauce and removed the lids to evaporate the liquid. Besides chili, there was yogurt for dipping raw vegetables, whole wheat bread and fruit. Lemonade, pop, and beer, were offered as well as large bowls of popcorn called *poporopo*.

We were lucky with the weather as it had rained heavily the day before, but the music was at such high volume it was hard to hear ourselves talk. Goody-Two-Shoes would have liked it! I had lunch with a young black volunteer and her parents who had lived in Tacoma while she was going to high school. The father was currently now president of a community college in Arizona. Joyce's site was up north and another volunteer had told me that, unfortunately, she had not been well-treated by some of the Guatemalans.

Back home, while I was trying to work in my room with the evangelical talk show turned to high volume just outside, Goody-Two-Shoes was waiting on customers in the farmacia. I turned the radio down and she came out and turned it back up. Not to be defeated, I brought it to her and sweetly told her she could hear it better when it was in the same room with her. I had noticed the volume was considerably lower when Chusita was home.

SANTOS, THE IRATE young grandmother of the baby adopted by the missionary couple, now had a twelve-day-old baby girl. When I stopped by, the mother said she was concerned about the way the baby's navel was healing. I mentioned it to Linda who suggested it could be infected and a doctor should see her and the baby.

Several days later, I carried the baby, with Santos and five of her children trailing behind, to the health center. Linda was rude and barely gave her the time of day. I examined Melinda and I couldn't see any sign of infection. Later, when I asked Linda why she wasn't nicer to Santos she replied, "Because she is irresponsible." This was truly not the real Linda.

I told Santos I would pay her way to the hospital in Jalapa, but she was to bring only the baby. The nurse at the hospital was a friend of Linda's and ushered us into the examining room. I had read Santos a story in Spanish from my teaching material about a woman who did not produce enough milk and the doctor confirmed what I had said. She was to drink a lot of liquid in addition to milk and Incaparina. He prescribed a special soap for the baby that we bought at the drugstore, and I bought her two bags of powdered milk and two large packages of Incaparina. In all I spent thirty-two quetzales.

THE FOLLOWING MORNING I worked in the school garden where carrots, beets, radishes, cabbage and broccoli had been "born," but not the watermelon. Fire ants again necessitated long pants and garden gloves with rubber bands around the wrists and ankles.

That afternoon at the women's group at Elinora's house, her daughter-in-law brought out a brand new Brother's sewing machine her husband had brought from the U. S. The women said they would like me to teach them to sew. To my relief, nothing was said about Uncle Pedro.

WE HAD A *DESPIDIDO*, or going away party, for Michelle and June and Barry at Michelle's house. I had volunteered to do the cooking and planned to serve chicken curry from *Sunset's Soup and Stew* book that I had always wanted to try. All the ingredients were available at the market except yogurt that Barbara brought from Guate.

Trina, a nurse and fairly new volunteer, helped me shop for cardamom, ginger, cinnamon, cloves, garlic and onions, which we cooked with the yogurt and chicken. We steamed a great pot of rice and served the curry with toppings of grated coconut and mango chutney. I had baked croissants the day before in my improvised oven and we had watermelon for dessert.

June was pregnant and I had knitted a white sweater for the baby on which I had embroidered a quetzal bird. Barbara had brought a new trainee named Dana from Texas who would be working in 4-H.

While Tina and I were shopping we ran into Don Billet and his bride, Carolina, who told us schools might be closed in September because of the political situation. Rios Mont was staging rallies and getting support. He was running as an Evangelical Christian but had been directly involved in some of the country's worst atrocities. In a previous election, some children had been kidnapped after they left school. I absolutely could not see how Rios Mont could have the ability to close schools.

AT HOME I PLANTED MY OWN GARDEN, having paid Arnoldo to dig up the space and spread manure. Goody-Two-Shoes was sure it should have leaves spread on top, and I shouldn't have followed her advice. I picked up a basket full of leaves from a tree that was obviously a legume and would contain nitrogen, but whatever it was, was like spreading poison oak on my garden. I had burning blisters inside one arm and on both hands. Calamine lotion and cortisone made it hurt more, as did Avon cream and an antibiotic. The next two days I had more blisters and the third day one huge one.

I walked up to school to talk to Aida who confirmed that school could be over in September. Afterwards, I checked on Santos, who popped out a breast and squeezed it to show me there was no milk. All the food I had bought was gone, obviously she had fed it to her children. I gave her my Peace Corps vitamins, but the situation seemed hopeless.

Another security meeting was held in our area, and when I changed busses at the highway, I noticed Dave, a new volunteer who had taken over at Buck's site. Dave had had an interesting life. His father, whom he never knew, was Syrian, and Dave was brought up by his mother. He was obviously bright, had worked his way through college, taught English in Iran, and served in the Peace Corps in Ethiopia and Belize. His Belize experience ended when he fell out of a mango tree and broke his hip.

We had omelets at a hotel in Jutiapa and then went to a market where I found a package of beef steak tomato seeds different from the small kind in our market. I felt they would do well with the heat, provided I could water them.

The group from Mateque were already at the hotel. Todd, the assistant director, outlined places to avoid. Gangs had robbed the early busses to Puerto Barrio and even though the police had added armed guards, one had been shot. The worst happening was the recent murder of an American who had been beheaded up in the Petén where he and his wife ran a bed and breakfast. The usual volcanoes were off limits because of terrorists. Latin America had had more rapes and female harassment than any other Peace Corps locations.

After that unpleasant news, we were served lunch and saw a video someone had recently taken of Guatemalan volunteers and their work.

SERGIO WANTED US to visit a school for developmentally disabled children in the capital. The school was located in an affluent section of the city and most of the children had Down's Syndrome. We were impressed that it was well-staffed, had small classes, both speech and physiotherapy, and a pre-vocational unit for older students. Money pledged for a Peace Corps "Run" would go to the school.

I told Sergio about Santos and he gave me the name of someone working at the Nestles plant I could contact in hopes of getting her some free formula. My interview there was totally unsuccessful, confirming my opinion of that company. Explaining that Santos, with no income or husband, twelve children including a newborn, was unable to breast feed, I hoped he would give me a case of formula. His answer was negative and he said that Santos should be breastfeeding, even though I said we had tried everything possible to establish her milk supply. When I told him the baby could die, he said there was nothing he could do about it.

Returning home, Chusita said she had heard a congressman from Jalapa had been killed on his way to Guatemala City to attend a legislative session. Later, I read in the paper the congressman and a friend were both shot by an assassin in their car in Jutiapa, where we had just been at the security meeting.

IRMA, THE JANITOR, came to my house to ask me if I could get diarrhea medicine for her husband. I was not able to hand out amoebae prescriptions but was able to give her a package of rehydration preparation. She said she badly needed money and asked if she could do my laundry. She seemed to have a source of water and I happily accepted. Francesca indicated she was ready to start a bakery if I would help build the oven. We talked to Maria who had built a number of them and enlisted her help. I said I would pay 135 quetzals if she would order the materials and have the base built. Francesca had grown children both in Canada and the U.S., a married daughter in town, and a girl still at home who was either retarded or had severe learning problems, as she was fourteen and still in the first grade.

As I trudged up to Carmen I thought about a Peace Corps volunteer in Malawi I had read about who spent his time traveling around the country doing puppet shows on public health. He even had the backing of the country's president. I wasn't a puppeteer, but I could write radio jingles as public service announcements that perhaps could be broadcast.

When I got home, I sat on the patio and wrote a song about vaccinations to the tune of *Jingle Bells* which briefly said, *"With vaccinations we maintain our health for life and eliminate measles, polio, DPT and TB."*

That weekend I had breakfast with June and Barry and helped them clean out their house. Their gas stove sat on concrete blocks and even though they were good housekeepers, we killed several dozen cockroaches when we took apart the bricks. I inherited their spices and marking pencils. I would miss them when they left.

It was fun making two puppets by cutting out the heads from a cardboard box and slipping a stick between the front and back. The hair was yarn and I painted features on the faces. I would tell a story about two girls the same age who had not met before and wondered why one was bigger than the other and had so much more energy until they compared their respective diets.

When Carlito and I walked up to Marina's house where June had built the oven, he picked up a rock and threw it at a pig on the road ahead of us. He was puzzled when I scolded him for hurting the animal. Kindness to animals was not a value in his culture.

We helped Marina bake four banana cakes. She had bought a package of frosting mix, and I hoped she could keep the flies off her cakes. On the way down the hill a man showed Carlito the tail of a black and white snake which he said was very large and good eating. A young boy stopped me and thanked me for the scholarship he and two girls had received which enabled them to attend seventh grade.

In 4-H we cooked borsch, as both beets and cabbage were always available in the market. Besides school girls, often young women with babies attended. One of them was Alba, who came with a year-old-boy and a girl the age of Goslier. I took a good look at the baby, and although she had chubby cheeks, the rest of her was painfully thin. Linda thought she was a candidate for the children's hospital; however, in looking at her eyes, both Linda and I could see the child had symptoms of zeropthalmia in one eye and needed immediate attention or she would lose her vision. Mario had lectured extensively on this, the cause being a lack of vitamin A and preventable. It goes from one eye to the other very quickly and the results are irreversible. Alba had been feeding the baby sugar water instead of milk. She was taken to Jalapa immediately and at least one eye was saved. I was thankful she and her mother had been at 4-H that day.

That night it was so hot I left my door open. About midnight Goody-Two-Shoes happened by and dutifully shut it. I shouted, "I want my door open or I would have shut it," which I was sure made her jump.

June had given me their solar oven which is supposed to be the panacea for Third World countries. It was constructed of a cardboard box, painted black and had a foil reflector on top. I heated red beans for chili on the stove and put them hot in the oven before I left for Piedra del Fuego to talk to the students about eye care. On the way back I was picked up by a man in a truck who, like many of the men around there, had worked in Stamford, Connecticut.

It was still hot and I collapsed in the hammock and read *War and Peace* before I left for my women's group at Petronia's. There didn't seem to be anyone around, which was unusual. Then Wilma appeared with her mother, Petronia, who sadly told me Rosa's baby had died the day before of diarrhea. Walking to her house, I told her how sorry I was. Nixon was as dirty as ever, the younger boy still had the sniffles, and the vicious dogs snarled and growled.

Back home I checked my beans which should have been nicely done after ten hours in the cooker, but it took two more hours on my gas stove.

Solar cooking was supposed to be the answer for conserving fuel, but it didn't work for me.

I baked a carrot cake and covered it with cream cheese frosting, which I carried over to Linda and Alfonso. Carlito looked most peculiar with only a fringe of hair, and his head appeared to have been shaved. "What have you done to this child?" I asked. Linda said he had acquired lice the day he played with Marina's son when we baked the banana cakes.

AUGUST SEEMED PARTICULARLY HOT. Big gray clouds came up every afternoon, and we would hope for rain, but it didn't come.

We had a good session up at Carmen where we cooked potato soup. My charla was one way of determining whether or not a child was malnourished, by measuring his arm with a tape measure. We discovered two youngsters needing to come down to the puesto.

That night I came up with two more public service announcements. Sung to the tune of *She'll Be Coming 'Round the Mountain*," it said, "*When you have a cough, cover your mouth, don't make others sick. When you sneeze, cover your mouth. Spitting on the floor is ugly.*"

The last one was to the tune of *The Happy Wanderer* about wearing shoes to avoid hookworm. I needed someone who could sing and play the guitar to record them for me.

The ditties would have worked well on busses, but I didn't have that kind of courage, let alone musical talent. Often salesmen stood at the front of the bus before it started and gave sales pitches for vitamins, Lifeboy soap, etc. Someone knew a volunteer who did nutrition talks on busses, but I hadn't the chutzpa.

ROXANE SEEMED TO HAVE FADED AWAY without a good-bye. Alicia and I decided she had done such a poor job she most likely would have to repeat her public health residency.

Our new doctor's name was Cézar, and he was Protestant, which pleased both Chusita and Pablo. He came to my house and asked me to take him around town and introduce him to folks. He planned to talk on denge fever for his first session with midwives and health workers.

I TOOK A BOX OF POWDERED whole milk to Santos to show her how to make a formula for the baby. Beginning with, "We always wash our hands before we prepare formula," she said there was no soap in the house. I showed her how to rub salt on the nipple to remove old mildew and said, "The bottle and nipple must be boiled before each use or the baby will become sick." We looked for a pan for sterilizing and there were two. One contained beans, and the other had a hole. By tipping the pan with the hole, I could get enough water to cover the bottle and it was boiled at least once.

We added the proper amount of milk to the water plus a little sugar and some oil. Melinda would have to be a tough cookie to survive, I thought.

On the way back I passed a sad little procession. Over the church loud-speaker Pablo announced that a baby had died and the services were to be held that morning at 9:00. The group carried a tiny coffin while singing a mournful song on the way to the church. Other deaths were announced on the radio from Jalapa, preceded by the funeral march and then a list of the deceased.

It was interesting listening to Voice of America on shortwave. The an-nouncer was advising all Americans in Kuwait to be ready to leave as soon as the borders and airport were open. Another advisory said Iraq had told the embassy to close and people were urged to stay in their homes and not try to escape through the desert.

ONE MORNING LINDA and I did vision screening for grades one through three in Llano Grande. At least twenty children needed to sit in the front row, and six definitely needed glasses. I was glad Linda felt well enough to show me how to do this. For children who hadn't learned their letters, we had them point in which direction a figure went. The next day I checked students in grades five and six and only a few needed to be in the first row and, in my opinion, no one needed glasses. I strongly suspected children with vision problems did not do well and dropped out of school early.

I was eating radishes from my garden. The broccoli was a foot high but infested with green worms exactly the color of the leaves. Commercial broccoli grown nearby was heavily sprayed. I saw young boys with spray cans fastened to their backs with no masks or any protection from the pesticide. Afterwards, they washed out the containers in the river. I didn't spray my broccoli and the worms won.

At times I didn't know why I bothered to raise vegetables. Chusita let the chickens out of the pen and they demolished my chard and all the new tomato plants. I tried to thin the carrots and ran into a nest of fire ants. Even with gloves I had bites on my wrists that lasted the better part of a week.

One day there was a very pregnant woman in the patio at my house. I asked when the baby was due and she replied, "*Horita*" (now). She said she wasn't in pain. Later she disappeared into the back bedroom and in the morning several girls brought her food. The baby was a seven-and-a-half-pound girl. I never saw the father visit. When I told Chusita that in the United States fathers often took part in the delivery, she replied, "Not here."

I WAS A LITTLE EARLY GETTING to my women's group at Terrones and watched a soap opera on television with Tina and her sister-in-law while we waited. There was a funny, older, chubby woman named Piedad, which I eventually figured out meant piety. Piedad enjoyed cooking and generally wangled more food to take home than the other woman. When she helped me prepare coconut pudding, I knew she put too much water in the powdered milk, the eggs were chunky instead of smooth, and it was a little scorched on the bottom, but the women declared it delicious and ate every drop.

LINDA AND HER HUSBAND and I planned a picnic at the park where Barbara and I had enjoyed swimming. I mixed up a potato salad and packed wieners and buns, carrot sticks and watermelon. Several months before, Alfonso had bought a truck, so we didn't need to rely on the bus. He invited a friend who came without his wife or children and on the way purchased one gallon of gas.

Alfonso took Carlito to the children's pool, where he was terrified of the water. After Linda and I changed into our suits, Alfonso swam with his friend and paid no further attention to the boy. Linda could not swim and

172

we played in the water with Carlito for awhile and I then had a chance to swim in the big pool.

We found the remains of a fire someone had left and roasted hot dogs and ate our picnic lunch. Afterwards, the men swam again, paying no attention to either of the children. Linda and I pushed Carlito on a swing and encouraged him to go down a slide, which he did with caution. Apparently Alfonso had a good time, as he suggested we have another picnic in October for Carlito's birthday, and he volunteered to bring meat for a barbecue.

That night I made a bowl of popcorn and ate an apple while I began *One Hundred Years of Solitude*. It impressed me as a strange book and I wondered why it rated a Nobel Prize. I was sorry to have finished *War and Peace*.

While eating lunch the next day, a man came up from Monjas to ask me about doing a latrine project. I told him I would need to talk to my supervisor and asked for a letter telling him what he needed from me. He knew 180 families in the area that were without them, but I wouldn't be there to see the project through. If Dave, the closest Peace Corps volunteer, wasn't willing to take over Buck's project, he wouldn't finish mine.

Every night it rained and the roads again were gummy with mud that stuck to our shoes, making the health center hard to keep clean. I hired Abner to pick off the green worms on my broccoli in hopes there would be some left.

Whenever I cooked, the minute I turned my back I needed to look out for Dobie or the cat who often sat by my stove hungrily watching me. One time the cat knocked the lid off a pan of cooked chard which he began to eat. This time I was soaking chard in an iodine solution so I would need to cook it only until tender. As neither the dog nor the cat were in sight, I went to my room. A few minutes later several chickens had wandered over and flown up to help themselves.

Eloisa ASKED ME if I would like to go on a pastoral call with them. She and her husband and a woman about my age climbed the hill to Carmen and took a path through a pasture. We climbed over a seven-foot fence and arrived at the poorest place I had seen yet. Living there was a sad girl of fourteen who cared for her seven-year-old retarded brother. The beds were made of limbs from small trees and the mattresses of cornhusks. She seemed embarrassed that we were there. The mother had died four years before and the father was an alcoholic. Eloisa kept telling her how much fun they had at church and that if she came down the hill to attend, they would find shoes and clothes for her.

Later, we called on the mother of a week-old baby and then a teenage girl who had such severe epileptic seizures she was bedridden.

I left to talk to Santos whose house was on the way home. Besides being concerned about the baby, neither her eighteen-month-old nor her granddaughter were walking, but scooted around on the dirt floor or in the yard. None of the older children attended school. I decided, if necessary, I would get the children to an orthopedic doctor.

During dinner there was another advisory on Kuwait on Voice of America. "We know these days are difficult and take courage, but your government is behind you and doing all we can to bring you back to your families."

AT THE HEALTH CENTER, I swept the floors. Apparently Linda felt it was too costly to have Irma come every day. She had been having her wash her dishes and clothes and care for the baby in addition to her cleaning job. Linda asked if I would talk to Irma and ask if she would work two hours for ten quetzals (less than two dollars) and asked me how much I would pay. I said I would match that and put in an extra ten each month.

That morning I talked about nutrition to two pregnant women, one expecting her eleventh child. A sad little girl with a large head came in who was losing her hair. At nineteen months she weighed only fifteen pounds.

That afternoon was 4-H where we cooked browned rice with Protemas soy substitute, onions, chili peppers and seasonings, which made a good and inexpensive dish.

MY NEXT PLANS for school were to have a community clean-up day. I had the students draw a map of Llano Grande and we talked about ways the town could be made cleaner. Maria's husband gave me three oil drums, and I planned to punch holes in the bottom to keep them from being stolen for containers, paint them green and letter "LLANO GRANDE BASURA" to use for trash cans.

School cleanup day

After 4-H "Cloob" I planted more broccoli, tomatoes, beets, radishes, lettuce and melons, hoping that with the rain we were having, the seeds would germinate. I managed to catch one of the hens that was loose and throw her back in the hen house, but a second eluded me.

In the front yard of the puesto was a twelve-by-twelve foot planter box in which Linda had planted zinnias and some canna lilies. She had had someone pull them out as fire ants had overrun the planter. I borrowed a hoe from Maria, which like most tools there had handmade handles, and it promptly broke. I asked Alfonso if he would wedge it back for me, but he was too busy playing cards and said, "*Mañana.*" As he said, the next day he took Linda to the doctor in Guate and later told me the handle couldn't be fixed. I then borrowed a shovel from Maria and finished the job. Ants foamed out of their nests, some having wings. I managed to stay clear and stamp my feet, only getting a few bites.

October 1990

*F*riends from home came to visit for two weeks. Pat and Bob McCain, their daughter Robin, and my long-time friend Catherine flew in to Guatemala City in the rain around 9:00 P.M. The next morning we headed for Antigua and then Lake Atitlán. We visited a church and museum called San Francisco where we viewed a Brother Pedro's hair shirt, underwear and other artifacts. We grandmothers bought smocked dresses for our granddaughters and had dinner at a charming hotel built around a patio. Being the rainy season, the skies opened up.

Atitlán is considered one of the most beautiful lakes in the world. Nearly all tourists visit there, and the Indians sell woven blouses, pants, bags and linens. There were lovely embroidered pieces in vivid colors typical of Guatemalan art.

A number of restaurants serve excellent food, and the flowers, shrubs and trees and the indigenous men and women in their *traje* (native dress) make the whole scene seem unreal.

We bartered for a boat the following day to take us twelve kilometers down the lake to a town where Felix, a Polish architect, had built a hotel he called *La Terraza*.

Made of stone, the hotel was terraced up from the lake with patios, a wide veranda, and attractive rooms that had hot showers and wool blankets. The town, San Antonio Palopó, is a weaving town built above the lake. The people all dressed alike, the boys like their fathers, and the girls like their mothers, as do most of the various Mayan people.

Heading for Guate and then Jalapa, we stayed at my usual hotel there. Bob was not impressed with the accommodations, but I had been away

Flood time

from home long enough to appreciate just a clean bed, bug-free room, and hot shower, even though it didn't resemble a Hilton. I reminded him we were in the Third World.

We toured Jalapa and the open market, buying food for the next few days. I took them for a walk around town and to the puesto, where Linda was not particularly friendly.

Crossing the river on the way to Piedra del Fuego, we all took off our shoes as the river was high. My friends helped with vision screening, and I talked to the father of a cross-eyed boy and the mother of a nearsighted girl urging them to bring the children to the health center.

Since that was my poorest school, I was surprised that all the students that day wore brown skirts or trousers and yellow shirts. It was the first time I had seen any students wear uniforms.

The following day we left for Guate and then flew to Tikal to the Mayan ruins, which are located in a tropical jungle of mahogany, cedar, palm and chiclet trees. We saw woodpeckers, spider monkeys and a tarantula, but I was disappointed there were no toucans or macaws. The vast temples dating from before the time of Christ made these ruins the most spectacular of any I had seen in Guatemala. No one knows what ended their way of

177

life. Our guide felt the people grew tired of being slaves or possibly the land wore out from overuse.

From Tikal we flew to Belize. Guatemala has never recognized the border, claiming the country still belongs to them. There were a number of British soldiers, although the country had been independent for at least ten years. Belize City was dirty with houses on stilts and open sewers and we observed "Crips and Blood" gang signs painted on buildings. Although most of the populace was black, they spoke Spanish; however, we were told English was taught in schools.

The King George Hotel was elegant, and we swam in their pool and had several outstanding meals before taking a small boat to Caye Calker where we stayed in a tropical hotel on the beach, spending two days snorkeling and swimming.

BARBARA MET ME IN GUATE where we did some shopping before returning home via Jalapa. At the yardage store, I could not believe my ears when the clerk told me Linda had died and the funeral held two days before. Barbara came out of another store and we ran into Chusita who confirmed the terrible tragedy.

According to Chusita, Linda had gone to the farmacia and bought rat poison, explaining there were rats at the puesto. Cézar had gone on an errand on his bicycle and Alfonso somewhere in his truck when Linda, with Carlito and the baby in the room, ingested the rat poison. Afterwards, he told someone, "My *mamacita* (little mother) swallowed some pills." When she was found, it was too late. It must have been a terrible way to die.

Barbara and I spent the night in Jalapa and thought about poor little Linda the whole time. Even though she had been receiving psychiatric help, I wondered if she had shared her problems if it would have made a difference. Besides, Linda had a beautiful baby, a husband who loved her, little Carlito, and a scholarship for Hispanic nurses for further study in Washington, D.C., to look forward to.

When I returned home, Alfonso and Carlito had left and I never saw either of them again. Linda's family blamed Alfonso, and Irma said Alfonso blamed her for not being of more help. I was devastated.

Above the door of the puesto Maria had hung a white funeral bow. I sent a telegram to Sergio, who in return wired both Linda's mother and me. It said, "I lament deeply the irreparable loss of Linda. We believe firmly Guatemala loses a valiant person and we share your pain."

My garden club from home had sent enough money to send two girls to junior high in Monjas for the next year. I had chosen Flor de Maria (flower of Mary) and another girl named Marlena. I wanted to take their pictures to send to the women in Tacoma and asked Marlena to run over to Flor's house to ask her to come to the 4-H for the picture. She returned saying Flor was *muy occupado* (busy). We found Flor at home wringing out clothes, looking tearful.

Linda's funeral wreath

She said there wasn't enough money for her to take the bus to school, but I told her we would find a way.

MARIA'S HUSBAND took the three garbage containers in his truck, and we placed one by the school and one outside the puesto. I had wanted the third at the fork in the road where there was always trash on the ground around Gloria's mother's tienda, but Augustina said, "No." We put it instead by the farmacia.

That day the whole school from first graders through sixth picked up trash and were rewarded by each receiving a ball point pen. I had thought about having the ice cream man come up, but had had enough experience to know some children would manage to get two or three cones and some would be left out. I had each teacher hand out pens.

The teachers asked what plans I had to empty the overflowing containers. I talked to the mayor who offered to take care of them and could dump the contents in the river, to which I emphatically said, "No!" I don't know where he took them but they were emptied.

179

That afternoon Cézar and I walked around town getting health data on various families and later cleaned out the puesto. He took all the posters down from the walls. Linda and Alfonso's room was filthy.

STEPHANIE HAD GIVEN ME instructions for getting to her village in the coffee country, Tukuru, which meant "Call of the owl" in Kekchi. I took a bus to a place called San Julian and waited an hour in the mist. Just as the bus came it really began to rain, and after a two-hour ride, the driver let me off in front of Stephanie's house.

Her site was one of the beautiful spots in Guatemala, where everything was green and tall trees had been left standing. There were African tulips with bright orange blooms, orchids, and Spanish moss hanging from great hardwoods. A swiftly flowing river passed in back of her four-room house. The back yard had been cut with a machete which she mentioned was necessary because of snakes. The river, which looked pristine, often contained waste—such as bandages and placentas—from the hospital upstream.

She was fortunate in having her pila inside, and because of a fire she had had with her gas stove, she did all of her cooking in an adjacent room on the floor with wood, placing the pot on bricks.

After drying out from the short walk from the bus to her front door, we ate lentil soup, cheese and homemade brown bread.

We visited Stephanie's future in-laws across the street. Mario, her *novio* (boyfriend), was attending teacher's college and was not there. He had four brothers—five, seven, nine and fifteen—and a baby sister. The three oldest, along with Mario, picked coffee as soon as school was out. Mario was able to pick 100 pounds on a good day, for which he was paid under two dollars. The father was over seventy and unable to work. The mother, who was indigenous, was gracious and friendly. Stephanie and Mario planned to build her a kitchen as soon as school was out.

The next day we were invited to the home of a woman who was "Mom" to all the volunteers. Stephanie had told her she wanted her to meet a "grown up" volunteer. She fed us a breakfast of bananas and sour cream, rolls and coffee, all of which were delicious.

At the school we showed three classes filmstrips I had brought on care of the teeth. All of the children spoke Spanish, although Kekchi was their first language. Stephanie said she had talked about a child to a teacher in Spanish who spoke to him in Kekchi and the boy relayed the information in a third tongue to his mother who lived high in the mountains.

At the hospital where Stephanie worked, the usually inebriated doctor was absent. There were only three adult patients—two very pregnant women and a third sitting in the corner with an I.V. needle in her arm.

Unlike the malnourished children at San Juan Sacatépequez, all the patients were up and about. Most of them were five to seven years in age. They were as small as two-year-olds—however, bright-eyed and stocky. One little boy had trouble walking because of swollen feet due to protein deficiency. A mischievous little girl had only the sight in one eye, like the baby in my village, due to insufficient vitamin A. Another child had the light hair and long eyelashes, symptoms of kwashiorkor.

The children had no toys, and Stephanie asked if my son, Jeff, could bring a frisbee when he came in December. I made a mental note to have him bring sturdy table toys as well.

These youngsters had only been in the hospital for a couple of months and would recover. If only their parents had brought them in earlier, they would not have had to be hospitalized, provided there was enough food at home.

Stephanie had made drawings for *Pepe and Patricia*, and we spent the remainder of the day illustrating the book. I told her I felt like a monk reproducing drawings for a manuscript in medieval times. Later we walked to Tukuru to buy marigolds to bring to Doña Pepita who had invited us back for dinner. Stephanie baked a marble cake in a ring mold in her improvised oven, and the cake looked and tasted as if she had had a modern electric stove.

When I left, Stephanie rode with me as far as Tactic where an attractive volunteer in agriculture from our training group had a rabbit-raising project. Rabbits are a good source of protein and the babies can be sold in a month for five quetzals each; however, they must be caged and fed special food.

As nearly all the people in Llano Grande let their animals run free to forage, I wondered how many of them would buy rabbit food. Later, when I mentioned it to Sergio, he said Guatemalans don't like to kill their pets. I recalled I had never seen anyone in my village show any kindness to an animal or qualms about their demise.

181

I WANTED TO SEE LINDA'S MOTHER, Carman. Before going, I looked for hibiscus plants but was unable to find any and settled on two rose bushes, one red and one yellow. A taxi took me to her house with instructions to return two hours later.

I told Carman the roses were for her to plant in order to remember Linda, and when they bloomed to remind her that her daughter had loved flowers and that I had loved Linda. We held each other a long time, tears streaming down our faces. Carman showed me Linda's room. The funeral wreaths were on the wall along with her college diploma and graduation picture. I played with Goslier until my taxi came.

A LETTER FROM THE CANADIAN WOMAN I had met in the capital, whose daughter had spent time in Cuba, sent the song she had promised. The school children sang, "All the teeth are soldiers standing straight and strong. Brush them like a soldier cleans his rifle. They can grind corn like a soldier grinds the enemy. Scrub the gums away and spit as though getting rid of the U.S. invaders at the Bay of Pigs. All the children of the world must brush, rinse and spit so that they will all have bright smiles to greet each other." My tooth song was pale by comparison!

FRANCESCA WAS FRUSTRATED by our oven. She had mixed a huge batch of sweet bread and found the oven hadn't heated enough to bake. I could see the heat was escaping from the door which wasn't tight and the wood was wet. Using my oven thermometer, and some dry weed, we got the heat up to 350 degrees and baked another pan full. The bread was brown enough, but she was not happy. Her neighbor had heated up her big beehive oven and we raked out the coals and baked French bread with the reserved heat. It was the best French bread I had ever baked.

A traditional oven does not have a door and I could understand why people didn't comprehend the importance of a door on our ovens. Francesca said she would not be able to get dry wood for several weeks, but she would have a better door made.

ONE SUNDAY MORNING I met Liesl in the capital for breakfast. Barbara had taken an earlier bus back to Mateque and Liesl talked me into going to a self-defense class one of the volunteers conducted Sundays at a park. The leader had a black belt in karate and counted in Japanese before we did warm-ups and thrusts. He then sent us out to look for a weapon. I felt a failure at kicks and laughed when I thought of how surprised my sons would be if they could see their mother. I thought of the *ancianas* in China doing group exercises, but I was the only anciana that day.

While in town I needed to buy some travelers checks. Simple things like that took an incredible amount of time and I had to go to several banks and then pay five U.S. dollars for $312.00. The teller was a woman disgusted and disgruntled with Guatemala. She remarked that politicians stole, poor people begged instead of worked, and the Peace Corps had been in the country thirty years and nothing had changed. The only hope for her country, she said, would be to sterilize both men and women after one child. I finally got my checks.

I ATTENDED MY LAST BIRD count with Liesl. Catching a bus in Jalapa, we got off on the Pacific highway and waited for a Puerto Barrios bus. I had packed us a lunch which unfortunately was in my luggage that got stored in the compartment on the side of the bus. We were lucky to get seats and watched a push-and-shove between a drunk and two policemen who finally bopped the man on the head with a gun. Luckily for the drunk, he had a friend who calmed him down. There was no stopping for anything and we reached our destination after dark.

The electricity was off in the city, and we took a taxi to the cockroach hotel and found a sidewalk café where we ate grilled beef and salsa wrapped in flour tortillas. That night several drunk men told jokes outside our window.

We were up at 4:00 and ate the peanut butter sandwiches I had made for yesterday's lunch. We had planned to buy bread, fruit and cheese, but no stores were open.

Spending several hours walking down the middle of the river, we saw a lovely red summer tanager as well as a blue-gray one. But the prize was a nesting hummingbird who had built her tiny cup-shaped nest of lichens on a vine above the bubbling creek. Even though we saw her come to the nest and leave several times, none of us could identify her.

Feeling thirsty, we were surprised when a man along the bank gave us a coconut containing at least a liter of juice. The inside was soft like a boiled egg. We thanked him and turned to leave when his little boy came running after us with a big bunch of bananas. I was always touched at the many kindnesses shown to us by people who had so little. I found a grapefruit on the beach and we ate that as well. It was almost dark when we returned to the city by bus. We got out of wet shoes and the group enjoyed a fish dinner.

OCTOBER WAS WORLD-WIDE Food Month, recognizing that most people in the world are hungry. Last year the health and nutrition people marched in the capital asking for money and this year planned a "Run." I had received a letter suggesting some ideas of things we could do in our villages to remind people of the event.

Some of them were to have children draw posters, but our school was on vacation. Another was to have a healthy baby contest, which might have been a good idea if Linda had been there. A third was to see which farmer grew the biggest *camote* (a sweet potato) but that sounded obscene. I settled on buying some small orange trees which not only were blooming but had grape-sized fruit. I had talked to Pablo about World Food Day and explained I would like to do a presentation in church and then plant the trees in the churchyard.

That Sunday, I read to the congregation in Spanish from Genesis, the verses where God said, "Let the earth put forth vegetation, plants yielding seed according to their own kinds, and trees bearing fruit. . . . Behold, I have given you every plant-yielding seed which is upon the face of the earth, and every tree with seed in its fruit; and you shall have them for food." Alvaro, from agriculture, dug the holes and we planted the trees. I had told the congregation they were "a symbol of His care."

I HAD A DISTURBING TALK with Francesca. She seemed upset when I came to her house and mentioned she looked sad. She told me a young person had broken into her house and stolen the equivalent of ninety dollars. I asked her if she had talked to the police and

184

she said, "No," nor would she talk to the mayor, as the family of the person was angry and she was afraid. We set up a date for baking in her new oven for the following week.

It was time for our C.O.S. (close of service) Conference at a lovely resort up north past the Rio Dulce on Lake Izabal. Of the fifty-seven trainees that had begun two years before, we were down to thirty-five who had seen it through. One of the nurses attended and told us what to expect from our physicals and the regimen of pills we were required to take for malaria in order to kill any parasites we might be harboring. There was a session on reports we were required to write and our own evaluations of our Peace Corps experience.

The last day Barbara and I took a boat to Livingston where we had lunch with some other volunteers. Most of the inhabitants were black, the descendants of Caribs who settled there early in the conquest of the Americas and intermarried with former British slaves. I was taking a series of pictures of faces of Guatemalans and met an older black woman wearing a wide-brimmed straw hat on which sat about a dozen bananas. When I asked if I could take her photo, she angrily said, "No."

We took another boat to Rio Dulce and then an uncomfortable minivan to the highway. Our bus was stopped four different times—the passengers were searched for weapons. Generally, only men were told to get out, but the last time, women as well.

DR. POLONKO, THE CHIEF of the medical facility in Jalapá was technically my *jeffe* (chief). Sergio called a meeting of the nutritionists and nurses in the area to give reports. Christine, a nurse who had been in Guatemala longer than most of us, told about some of the people in her mountain village with active tuberculosis. She said she had brought them down to the hospital only to find they would not admit them and finally had taken them to a private doctor for treatment. After talking for nearly an hour, she ended by calling the medical people uncaring, unchristian and unprofessional. Sergio was plainly embarrassed by her outburst.

Sergio took us all out to lunch and then drove me home. Telling me he liked *Pepe and Patricia*, he wanted me to write more stories. With Linda gone, he felt, rightly, I hadn't enough to do. He also suggested I talk to Dr.

Polonko about working at the puesto in Monjas doing health education classes.

W E WERE AWARE at all times of the coming election. Headlines in the paper said the mayor of Jalapa had been shot the night before. Voice of America reported eight politicians had been killed recently in Guatemala and an election team was coming to observe the primaries. The final elections were to be held after the new year.

On a less serious note, I noticed a wonderful political poster announcing "PEPE FOR PRESIDENT" under which was a picture of a jolly fat man with a big smile and wearing a straw hat. On the side we were advised that Pepe did not rob, lie or cheat!

Sunday was election day and the bus made extra trips all day so Llano Grande residents could go into Jalapa to vote. I noticed Chusita voted, but had no idea who else took part.

It had become colder and the wind whistled through the cracks in the roof. The electricity was off and I barely had time to cook dinner. As there were no candles in the farmacia, I used a flashlight for working on my talk for another United Church Women's group, that year to be held in Llano Grande. Again, I would need to skip the last day of the yearly Peace Corps Conference.

The electricity was still off while I cooked vegetables on my gas stove to use in a food demonstration three days later. I could only hope they didn't spoil. I packed for three days in Guate for Thanksgiving.

Our host worked at the embassy. He and his wife were black, from Philadelphia, and said this was a second career for them both. Their home was close to our hotel, meaning we could walk. The other guests were mostly black and included marines and diplomatic service people.

A white-jacketed waiter served us drinks and dips. There was a cook in the kitchen, but our hostess supervised a Southern Thanksgiving dinner which, besides turkey, included collard greens and ham, turnips, homemade rolls and sweet potato pie.

The second year's conference seemed to have a more courteous group of volunteers. The vice council from the embassy said either candidate running for president would be acceptable to the United States. Someone asked if anything was being done about land reform and the answer was, "No."

The program was a fashion show of typical clothes worn in different areas, someone told jokes, and another volunteer sang and played the guitar. Each group presented a program on their work. I left in the middle of the afternoon, arriving in Jalapa five hours later, where I spent the night. The following morning I saw Argentina from Llano Grande on the bus, who reported the electricity there was back on.

THERE WERE AT LEAST SEVENTY-FIVE WOMEN at the church where I showed a film on good foods for babies and talked about the four rules for feeding young children. I made a cold fruit drink from Incaparia, pineapple, mashed bananas, and orange and lemon juice, as well as little pancakes of protemas and vegetables. I used three baskets showing foods from each group and demonstrated making both cooked vegetables and fruit into baby food. Afterwards, we played lotteria until it was too dark to see.

I was tired when I went to bed. There was a peeing bat in my room again who flew only at night. I never saw him because when I turned on the light, he always disappeared.

My week was spent talking to patients at the health center in Monjas on nutrition and pregnancy. It was difficult, as only the doctors and nurses knew me and none of the mothers were particularly interested.

As usual, my women's group in Terrones began with only a few. Gradually more adults and a number of school children filled the patio. I had brought macaroni, carrots and radishes for a salad; someone contributed eggs. Tina brought cream, vinegar and onions for the dressing. Everyone colored foods from the energy group I had traced on paper, and we concluded by playing *canasta revuelta* (fruit basket upset).

During the night it became warmer and began to rain, sounding like home. As a Pacific Northwesterner, rain is a part of my life. I had just finished *Bitter Fruit*, an account of a coup taking place in Guatemala during the Eisenhower administration to protect United Fruit and, ostensibly, the country from Communism. Our disgraceful meddling under the Dulles brothers caused incredible suffering from which Guatemala has never recovered; a shameful episode in American policy.

The next day it was still raining. Francesca and I had planned to bake bread, but she had not bought wood and it would have been wet, anyway.

187

She complained of a pain in her stomach and I gave her the Malox from my first aid kit. I had planned to go to 4-H in the afternoon but Maria was busy distributing bags of wheat and corn from Canada and the U.S. Agriculture Departments.

Cézar gave a talk on the treatment of burns to the health promoters. My contribution was to pretend he was an *estufa* (stove) to demonstrate how easy it was for a child to grab the handle of a pan upsetting boiling liquid on himself.

In Monjas I did my second health talk, showing a film on breast feeding. Again, it was difficult as the room was crowded with crying, sick babies and patients kept waiting literally for hours.

After waiting a long time for a bus, I learned there was another bus strike. I was lucky to hail a mini-van that took me to the Llano Grande turnoff and then caught a ride as far as Terrones. I left the projector at Elenora's house and walked home from there.

Francesca finally started a fire in the oven and the heat rose to 400 degrees, 'tho the oven smoked. We mixed both oatmeal and whole wheat bread and shaped the dough into rolls. I went to Carmen for my women's group where I played Fruit Basket Upset with the children, who laughed and laughed when I told them they were a cornflake or a tomato. Nixon actually smiled at me and his brother stood close to me, which he had never done before. Neither of the boys wore anything but T-shirts which I guessed made for less laundry. Poor Rosa, their mother, was pregnant again.

I wrote two more stories. Pepe and Patricia learned about caring for their teeth as well as good health habits. Both Cézar and Eloisa read them and corrected my Spanish, which I appreciated. The young, giggly, health promoters had a surprise party for Cézar with a cake, presents, and firecrackers accompanied by music from a radio someone had brought.

I was due in the capital for my close-of-service physical, but because of the country-wide bus strike wondered how I would get there. Luckily, one of Chusita's daughters and her husband and girls were visiting and offered me a ride in their car.

On Monday I arrived at the lab where I relinquished blood, urine and a stool sample. The next day was for teeth cleaning and a dental exam. When I told the dentist about Francesca's robbery, he said he would never inform the police as they expected payoffs, adding that anyone in the capital who had money banked it in the U.S.

The following day both Barbara and I were examined by the Peace Corps doctor, followed by a trip to the hospital for mammograms and EKGs. Charlie, the swimmer, was waiting in the nurse's office and said he had written two letters to the Pope concerning family planning. I never found out if the Pope responded.

JEFF, MY THIRD SON, who was beginning a master's program in psychology in Colorado, arrived the next day. We headed for Lake Atitlán and took a boat across the lake to Santiago, where the week before a tragedy had occurred. From a nearby army camp, drunken soldiers had been molesting townspeople. In retaliation, the mayor led a group of people armed only with rakes, sticks and hoes to the camp where the army fired into the crowd killing some and wounding a number of them. Nearly every house had a black bow above its door. This had been an area of terrorist activity, and at the city hall was a collága of pictures identifying those who had been killed, wounded or kidnapped. On the wall in the church were hundreds of crosses for those unfortunate souls. Ten years before, a much-loved American priest had been murdered on the steps of his church.

We made the trip by a small boat to Felix's hotel. He was visibly upset, telling us the town had destroyed his stone wall and lower gardens above the beach. We surmised the hotel property had taken away any beach rights the townspeople had enjoyed.

Jeff had spent two and a half years cycling by himself from Circle, Alaska, to Tierra del Fuego a few years before, and his Spanish was excellent. Some young girls became unpleasant and hostile when he refused to buy their weaving.

Heading for Chichicastenango, we splurged, staying at the beautiful Santa Tomas Hotel. Unfortunately, we were both feeling marginal, which was too bad as the food was excellent and the hotel a show place. Jeff and I both bought some belts. I was chagrined that he was able to bargain for a better price!

THE STEERING WAS NOT WORKING properly on the Llanó Grande bus, necessitating sitting on the curb in Jalapa while the

189

work proceeded. Marina, of the first oven project, and her little boy were on the bus, and to entertain him I read *Peter Rabbit* in Spanish which Pat McCain had brought me. William liked it, but one of the mechanics under the bus was absolutely fascinated and kept popping his head out. I hoped he was tending to his work. Most likely he had never before heard a story, and possibly couldn't even read.

After we were underway, Jeff was concerned that we might careen over the side of a cliff, but I assured him that other than a rather rickety wooden bridge which spanned the river, there were no cliffs.

IT WAS FUN SHOWING HIM my village, and because he was handsome, friendly, and fluent in Spanish, everyone liked him. We bagged CARE products, went to a women's group in Terrones and visited with people. Chusita was impressed that he helped me with the dishes.

IN GUATEMALA CITY, a note in my box at the Peace Corps office informed me I had acquired amoebas, and after reading about the side effects of the strong medicine, decided to wait until after Christmas to begin taking it. Jeff and I had breakfast with a group of volunteers, and he left for Antigua to study Spanish for a few days before heading for Mexico. Barbara, Liesl, Elizabeth, and Tom, a teacher from our training group, and I caught a bus for the border at Huehuetenango to go to Mexico City for Christmas.

It was a two-hour ride from Huehue to the border. All the bridges had armed guards to prevent them from being blown up by guerrillas. We then rode in another truck to wait for a bus for San Cristóbal, a lovely colonial city. We visited a fascinating museum and art studio begun by an archeologist couple who had devoted their lives to preserving the culture of the nearby Indians.

On to Palanque, beautiful ruins set in an emerald-green park. The only problem was that I was getting bronchitis again. Christmas Eve found us on a bus for Puebla. After Guatemala, the busses with their assigned seating, the paved highways and attractive cities which resembled Europe, made that part of Mexico seem affluent, clean and modern. We pulled into Puebla at 6:00 A.M. Christmas morning; a taxi driver found us a hotel, and

I was able to spend the day in bed.

Feeling better the next day, we rode to Cuernavaca where Barbara and I went shopping that evening. While she was charging her purchases, the electricity went off and the transaction was concluded by candlelight. We had dinner on a balcony overlooking a darkened street.

From Mexico City we took a bus to the ruins at Teotihuacán where we ran into Liesl who had left us several days before to meet her parents. They had reserved a place for us at the Quaker house, which was a relief, as we had no idea where to look for a pensión. The next several days were spent at museums, markets, and cathedrals and on my birthday, a wonderful trip through a canal the Aztecs had built for irrigation.

In the evening we four volunteers were asked by the Quakers to tell about our experiences in Guatemala. They were well-informed about atrocities and human rights, bluntly asking what we were doing to hasten land reform and expose the corrupt government.

I felt defensive explaining we were an arm of the U. S. State Department, invited to Guatemala to do our work, and expressly forbidden to become involved in Guatemalan politics. I had the feeling they were not impressed.

We left after breakfast for Taxco, the silver city, and then to Oaxaca where we boarded an all-night bus for Guatemala. We had breakfast at the border and drove through the southwestern part of the country I had not visited, passing rubber plantations, sugar cane and cotton fields. We had been told this was a drug growing and transportation region and was off limits to volunteers.

IT WAS GOOD TO GET BACK to dirty, smoky Guatemala City. As I boarded a city bus, two angry, unpleasant young women were standing just outside the door. Other than noticing they looked unfriendly, I thought nothing of it and took a seat near the back of the bus. Placing my gym bag on a rack, I set a cloth bag holding my camera and a lipstick in front of me. A young man called my attention to the fact that my Nikon camera was on the floor. I found the girls had slashed the bottom of the bag with a razor as I boarded.

I was on a regime of Flagyl and Yodoxim for twenty days to kill my amoebas. I had no symptoms and had been very careful about boiling drinking water and soaking raw vegetables in iodine. I concluded I had gotten them from a restaurant, or eating in someone's home. After finishing the pills, I was required to submit three more stool samples to the lab. If my purse were snatched, I felt the robber deserved what he would find!

BARBARA AND I WERE INVITED to visit Trina and Gary. We squeezed onto a crowded bus, lucky to find seats. Gary had said the town was founded in 1860 by people from San Juan Pinula, sixty miles away. We passed the foundations of a very old house and the remains of an aqueduct.

Trina worked as a nurse and was horrified at her Guatemalan counterpart who tossed dirty bandages on the floor and believed slices of rat to be a cure for diphtheria. Gary had a master's degree in agriculture and had worked as an extension agent. He was discouraged as he said the land was barely marginal for farming. More upsetting was that his one good representative had to leave town. When a drunk farmer with a machete was threatening him, a policeman came on the scene, was also threatened, and then shot and killed the farmer. The representative was forced to leave town as the drunk's family had a vendetta out for him.

Trina and Gary lived in a nice house consisting of two rooms connected by a patio. Their beehive oven was built in the wall and could be used as a fireplace. Trina asked me for a bread-baking lesson and we baked both brown bread and oatmeal raisin. She fixed burritos with beans and chopped vegetables. That night it was cold enough that two wool blankets felt good, in addition to a down bag. I didn't feel well; the amoebae medicine was upsetting my stomach.

Trina was Catholic and we attended mass on Sunday. The church was packed with parishioners standing on either side of the pews. The women had covered their heads with long pastel scarves. Looking over the congregation one saw a sea of color.

I RETURNED HOME on the eve of the Gulf War. The next day at Terrones, a man mentioned that the United States was at war and asked if I was worried that my house might be bombed? I explained that Iraq was on the other side of the world near the land where Jesus had lived, so I wasn't really worried about my house.

Francesca said she would have flour on Saturday, Flor said her father would allow her to attend school on the scholarship, and we had a new nurse to take Linda's job.

The nurse was male and named Ronnie. Friends of Linda's from Monjas had been coming in, but Ronnie got the job. Paulina came in and we determined Erika had grade-one malnutrition.

Only two weeks until it was time to go home. My last trip by bus to Jalapa was memorable. Because the bus originated in Llano Grande, our town had window seats. Later, another woman sat next to me, and as the bus filled along the highway, a woman got on who spoke to an attractive woman sitting in the front and then took a place next to my seatmate on the aisle. Suddenly, there were verbal fireworks between the two women, the Spanish being so fast I could hardly follow. Much to our horror, the woman in the front pulled a pistol from her bag and pointed at the woman screaming obscenities. We were all terrified. Chema, our fearless ayudante, grabbed the pistol, telling her it was not permitted, and he and another woman calmed her down, 'tho the insults continued. At the next stop, the pistol-packing passenger got off, and the bus proceeded to the police station to file a report. I surmised they had the same boyfriend, and when I asked Chema if the gun had been loaded, he assured me it was.

At MY HOUSE CREAM-COLORED bougainvilleas were blooming. Of all the colors—cerise, purple, pink and coral—I like white the best. It was amazing Chusita was able to grow so many flowers with so little water. The well never was finished; even when a Sears pump was installed, they could not draw any water.

I baked a batch of chocolate chip cookies with both Dobie and Gato sitting close-by licking their chops and hoping I would drop something. Meanwhile, across the street was a revival meeting going on with ear-splitting hymns and an hour of loud sermon, which I tried to drown out by playing Vivaldi on my tape deck.

At our last 4-H meeting we made peanut brittle and played a final game of lotteria. Fifty girls gave me farewell hugs and kisses. Marlena sadly told me she was unable to accept her scholarship as her grandmother was ill

193

and there was no one to care for her.

During the last week of January it was hot during the day and we were again short of water. There were huge cracks in the ground. The revival meetings lasted all week, the proceedings being amplified by two large speakers and lasted each evening until 10:00. I was glad I needed to go to the capital for two days, even though there was a note from the director telling all volunteers to stay away from Guate if possible and that Americans should not gather in groups because of possible terrorist activities.

I closed out my bank account, bought cardamom and saffron at the spice store, and some lovely handwoven fabric. Liesl took me to lunch at a Swiss pastry shop, and I took Trina and Gary to an Italian restaurant for dinner.

Trina told a terrifying story. She had had a meeting with the midwives in her area after which one of the women returned home, several miles up in the mountains. Two men who said they were working up there came to her home and asked her to fix them something to eat. When she complied, they demanded her money. Unfortunately, she had a pistol hidden in the kitchen and as she reached for it, one of the men chopped off her arm with a machete. The woman's six-year-old granddaughter escaped, screaming for help, but by the time help came, the men had left and the victim had bled to death.

A TRUCK FROM THE PEACE CORPS would be coming in a few days to pick up my belongings and take me to the capital. After a breakfast of cantaloupe and whole-wheat pancakes with blackberry sauce, I began packing. I had brought a large lidded basket for my quilt and other bulky items, and with my two suitcases, gym bag and backpack, I got everything ready to send home. Eloisa wanted my cookware and I gave her some clothes, although she was three times bigger around than I. Goody-Two-Shoes wanted my thongs and any kitchen items I had left, as she was being married soon. I left my sheets for Chusita and gave the church one hundred quetzals and fifty for a young widow and her son in the congregation.

OUT OF CURIOSITY, in the afternoon I attended the camp meeting where at least 200 people were clapping, stomping and singing. An eight-month-old baby clapped along with her mother. At dark, a movie was shown. Although it was in Spanish, the story took place in Japan where a teenage swinger lost her leg in a train accident, but was "saved" by a group of Christian young people. The audience wasn't very attentive and left en masse before the service was over.

I WAS INVITED TO DINNER at the parsonage on my last day. Eloisa had invited Alicia, Chusita, Goody-Two-Shoes, Alvaro from agriculture, and Gilda who cut my hair. Pablo and the three boys were included. Afterwards, each of them thanked me for working with the children. The group then sang in harmony, a hymn with which I was not familiar. In essence, it was *God Take Care of You*. Through tears, I told them I would always remember them and what a privilege it had been to be a part of their lives.

My last trip to Guate was uneventful, and Peace Corps had my ticket ready for me. The day I left, the plane was delayed six hours because the president was expected to arrive, which gave me time to take a taxi to an arts and crafts center to purchase an oil painting of a Mayan girl.

When the plane finally took off for Dallas and then fogbound Seattle-Tacoma, I knew part of me would always belong to Guatemala. Her government is corrupt, her problems are immense, but I loved the people whose lives I shared.

Margarita with village children

195

Epilogue, January 1992

A year later, I felt I needed to return. Llano Grande was as dirty as ever, and the only available water was what women could get from wells and carry in pans or buckets on their heads. There were cases of denge fever, and the whole country was terrified of a cholera epidemic. The newspaper stated it had caused 300 deaths at Lake Atitlán in the last four months.

Chusita said there was a great deal of "grippe" as well as malnutrition. She took me to visit a terribly anemic, thin, eighteen-year-old mother of two pathetically thin boys who were lying in a hammock. I agreed to pay for an iron shot for the mother as there was no medicine at the puesto. In Denver, on my way there, I had been given 100 dollars for food and medicine, and I was able to buy sixty pounds of dried whole milk and twenty pounds of Incaparina to be distributed.

"Margarita, how fat you are, and how white you are," everyone exclaimed. I had many *besos* and *brazos* (hugs and kisses). Maria sent over a bag of fresh broccoli, Irma, two duck eggs, and the most touching was a live chicken from Santos (which Chusita bought from her). Melinda was eighteen months old and, although thin, was an active little girl.

The best surprise was Maria Angelica who was neither walking nor talking when I left and was now running and smiling.

Chusita and I set up a bank account in Jalapa for scholarships for twenty students to attend junior high, and sadly, I said good-bye.